"The issues of injustice and racial discrimination must be faced head on. I have not yet seen a group study that challenges its participants at this level. Alvin Bibbs sets the bar high, urging readers to open their eyes to a world desperately in need of Christ's compassion. Beyond that, this provocative and insightful study leads participants into action in the ways of Christ. I can't recommend this experience highly enough."

BILL HYBELS, Senior Pastor of Willow Creek Community Church, and Founder of Willow Creek Association

Alvin C. Bibbs Sr.

with Marie Guthrie and Kathy Buscaglia

Changing Your World

Through Compassion,

Justice and Racial

Reconciliation

IVP Connect

An imprint of InterVarsity Press
Downers Grove, Illinois

InterVarsity Press
P.O. Box 1400, Downers Grove, IL 60515-1426
World Wide Web: www.ivpress.com
E-mail: email@ivpress.com

InterVarsity Press® is the book-publishing division of InterVarsity Christian Fellowship/USA®, a movement of students and faculty active on campus at hundreds of universities, colleges and schools of nursing in the United States of America, and a member movement of the International Fellowship of Evangelical Students. For information about local and regional activities, write Public Relations Dept., InterVarsity Christian Fellowship/USA, 6400 Schroeder Rd., P.O. Box 7895, Madison, WI 53707-7895, or visit the IVCF website at <www.intervarsity.org>.

All Scripture quotations, unless otherwise indicated, are taken from the Holy Bible, New International Version®. NIV®. Copyright ©1973, 1978, 1984 by International Bible Society. Used by permission of Zondervan Publishing House. All rights reserved.

Design: Cindy Kiple
Images: Nina Matyszczak/iStockphoto

ISBN 978-0-8308-2115-0

Printed in the United States of America ∞

Library of Congress Cataloging-in-Publication Data

Bibbs, Alvin C.
  Crazy enough to care: changing your world through compassion,
justice & racial reconciliation / Alvin C. Bibbs, Sr. with Marie
Guthrie and Kathy Buscaglia.
    p. c.m.
  ISBN 978-0-8308-2115-0 (pbk.: alk. paper)
  1. Christian education—Textbooks for youth. 2.
Compassion—Religious aspects—Christianity—Textbooks. 3.
Christianity and justice—Textbooks. 4. Race relations—Religious
aspects—Christianity—Textbooks. I. Guthrie, Marie. II. Buscaglia,
Kathy. III. Title.
  BV4647.S9B52 2009
  261.8071'5—dc22

2009000423

P	20	19	18	17	16	15	14	13	12	11	10	9	8	7	6	5	4	3	2	1
Y	25	24	23	22	21	20	19	18	17	16	15	14	13	12	11	10	09			

Contents

Introduction

Jesus—What Are We Following Him Into?

Activist. Rebel. Revolutionary. Who comes to your mind when you read these words? Do you think Jesus would make a top ten list in these categories? Most likely not. Yet, think about how the people of his day responded to Jesus' words and actions. Entire communities were turned upside down. Religious leaders felt threatened. Political leaders were baffled. Adversaries responded with rage. And followers gave up their lives for Jesus.

Jesus was passionate, intense and zealous. He challenged the idea that following God was predictable and rules-oriented. Jesus lived and breathed a faith in God that was fresh, freeing, personal and inclusive. He went so against the grain of his day that religious leaders thought he was . . . crazy.

What was Jesus crazy about? People. Jesus passionately reflected God's deep love for all people. His compassionate, just and reconciling acts blew the minds of the "religious" people of his day. Whether harassed by an angry mob or ridiculed for associating with social outcasts, he stopped and looked into the eyes and hearts of the people near him. He was crazy enough to care.

Whether you are a follower of Jesus or a spiritual seeker, what effect does Jesus have on you? What practical, tangible difference does following Jesus make in your life? Or, perhaps, what difference could it make? Regardless of where you are at on your spiritual journey, God's heart calls out to you through the life and words of Jesus.

This learning experience is all about understanding, receiving and passing on Jesus' outrageous compassion, justice and racial reconciliation. The twelve sessions in this guide are intended to take you deep into fresh knowledge about biblical Christianity. As the sessions progress, you are invited to open yourself up to radical encounters with people Jesus loves. You may want to keep a compassion journal throughout this learning experience.

During the next few weeks, you will encounter

OUTRAGEOUS IDEAS. How can Jesus transform my mind? How do I see things the way Jesus does? How can Scripture be my guide? What are my blind spots when it comes to God's fullest plan for my life?

INTENSE looks at my own INTERIOR. How can Jesus transform my emotions? How could the things that break God's heart break my heart?

VIBRANT ACTIONS God is calling me to take. How can Jesus transform my actions? If Jesus were in my shoes, how would he respond to people near me?

The prayers and activities provided in "Till We Meet Again" will help you in between sessions build on what you learned as a group. In addition, sessions 4 and 10 are opportunities to experience what you've learned in a real-world environment.

Jesus lived an intense and radical life for God. He calls you to do the same. Are you up for growing deeper in God's joy as you mirror his son? If so, get ready for an extraordinary encounter with God and the people he loves.

Suggestions for Group and Individual Study

SUGGESTIONS FOR MEMBERS OF A GROUP DISCUSSION

Group discussion is as good as the energy and commitment that you as a member bring to the group. The following suggestions are shared to assist you in preparing for and participating in your group discussion experiences.

- Expect your leader to provide insights on how to best prepare for your learning. In most cases, the best preparation is to open yourself to God's guidance through sensitive issues. Careful preparation greatly enriches your group discussion experience.

- See your leader as a facilitator and encourager, not a lecturer. Your leader's goal is to ask questions that are appropriately challenging. Each question found in this guide assumes a variety of answers. In many cases, there are no "right" answers. Questions push you to explore the topic and issues more thoroughly.

- Prepare to interact with the group and stay on the topic being discussed. This allows everyone to feel comfortable in group discussion. Listen attentively and be sensitive to other members of the group as they share what they are learning. Each member is in a different place of learning. You may be surprised by their insights and how they impact you.

- Affirm others during group discussion. Positive comments encourage hesitant members of the group to participate.

- Be careful to not dominate discussions. When we are eager to express our thoughts, we often get caught up in what we are saying and may leave little time for others to respond. You may find this happening to you as God teaches you many new things in this learning experience. By all means participate, but allow others an opportunity to share as well.

- Expect God to show up and teach you.

- Pray that you enjoy one another. Also pray that you find ways to take action individually and as a group upon completion of each session and your learning experience as a whole.

- Agree that anything discussed in the group is confidential and should not be discussed outside the group, unless specific permission is given to do so.

If you are the group leader, there are additional suggestions for you at the back of this guide.

SUGGESTIONS FOR INDIVIDUAL STUDY

While *Crazy Enough to Care* is best used as a group resource, it can be used for individual study as well. Adaptations you can make for individual study include:

- Review the appropriate leader's notes at the back of the book before beginning each session. These notes give you additional questions and exercises to enhance the learning experience.

- Pray as you begin each session that God will speak to you. Use the prompts in "Checking In with God" and adapt them for your individual prayer time.

- Adapt the instructions in each section for your individual use. It will enhance your experience to write your answers to the questions in a personal journal. Writing can bring clarity and deeper understanding of yourself and how God is teaching you and calling you to follow him through this learning experience.

- Use the "Till We Meet Again" section as a time to thank God for what you learned and pray about the applications that have come to mind. Consider debriefing your learning with a trusted friend or spiritual mentor in between sessions.

God's Radical
Heart-Change Plan
Am I Up for It?

CHECKING IN WITH GOD: OPENING PRAYER

Open up your time together by inviting God to join you as you seek to understand biblical compassion. Pray with your small group that you will know more fully that

- God is compassionate
- biblical compassion starts with receiving compassion from God

OUTRAGEOUS IDEAS

An Exercise in Compassion

Write the word *compassion* on the center of a large piece of paper. Take a moment for each person in the group to define *compassion* in three words or less:

> To me, compassion means . . .

Write each person's definition on the sheet of paper. Have one group member summarize what compassion means to the group.

> To us, compassion means . . .

At the end of this learning experience, your group will come back to this definition of compassion.

Discuss where and by whom you see your group's definition of compassion lived out daily.

God's Autobiography

Getting to know the real truth about people is one reason autobiographies are on bestseller lists. What's intriguing is whether or not their self-perceptions line up with the way other people see them.

Have you ever thought of the Bible as an autobiography? God uses words to detail a clear self-portrait. One of his key character traits, it turns out, is compassion.

> When he cries out to me, I will hear, for I am compassionate. (Exodus 22:27)

> The LORD is compassionate and gracious, slow to anger, abounding in love. (Psalm 103:8)

> Yet the LORD longs to be gracious to you; he rises to show you compassion. (Isaiah 30:18)

> The LORD is gracious and righteous; our God is full of compassion. (Psalm 116:5)

> Have mercy on me, O God, according to your unfailing love; according to your great compassion blot out my transgressions. (Psalm 51:1)

What is God telling you about himself through these verses?

How does your experience of God sync up with how he's described in these verses?

Jesus—Living, Breathing Proof of God's Compassion

God very specifically shows himself as compassionate in the New Testament, through the person of Jesus. Teaching in a synagogue, he unrolls a scroll of the Old Testament prophet Isaiah and quotes:

The Spirit of the Lord is on me, because he has anointed me to preach good news to the poor. He has sent me to proclaim freedom for the prisoners and recovery of sight for the blind, to release the oppressed, to proclaim the year of the Lord's favor. (Luke 4:18-19)

After the reading, he sits down and tells the people that these verses come true in him, basically saying, "I see you hurting people, all of you. I am all about justice and compassion. I am God and I'm here to free you."

Jesus spent the next three years living these words out. He healed the sick, taught about God's love, fed the hungry and poor, stood up for social outcasts and suffered for his friends.

When Jesus landed [from a boat trip] and saw a large crowd, he had compassion on them, because they were like sheep without a shepherd. So he began teaching them many things. (Mark 6:34; see also Matthew 14:14)

What does God show us about compassion through Jesus' example?

Intense interior

A Cleansing Compassion

Split up in groups of two or three. Take a few minutes to read this real-life story silently and answer the questions that follow.

As one of thirteen children, Amber grew up on the south side of one of the largest cities in the United States. At fifteen years old, she was in the custody of the state because her life was in disarray. By sixteen, Amber found herself pregnant and alone. She dropped out of school.

Amber lived on and off the streets. Addicted to drugs and alcohol, she traded her body to satisfy her addictions. She had another child and tried to balance raising her family alone while satisfying her need for drugs.

Twice she was unsuccessful at trying to end her life. Through

13

tears, Amber says, "I found myself in the shower, scrubbing my body, literally looking to be clean. I didn't know what it meant that you could be clean on the inside."

One day, Amber went to church because her children were begging her to go. Uncomfortable sitting in the church, she walked through the halls and came upon a leader talking to a group about forgiveness through Jesus' death on the cross. Amber said to the man, "You are a liar!" She couldn't imagine a God that forgives all things.

For seventeen years, God reached toward Amber, and one day she chose to grasp the hand of Christ, her Savior. God met Amber in the depth of her experience. He did not hold all that she had done against her but forgave her in the midst of her shame and pain.

Through God's hand, Amber's relationship with her kids was restored. One day, her daughter introduced Amber to a fourteen-year-old friend, who couldn't go back to school because she had a baby. Amber stepped in and helped with childcare. High school friends kept telling each other about "Ms. Amber," until Amber found herself caring for a dozen girls' children.

Today, God is using her as an executive director of a facility that provides childcare so that mothers can go to school. The families are also taught about a God of compassion and love.

When Amber looks around her, she sees real cleansing. "God reached down and pulled me out of the quicksand that I was in. I was crying out for help but no one seemed to hear me. God was the only one who could hear me and save me. He gently reached down and pulled me up and wiped me off. He provided for me and my kids."

God, in all his love, did clean Amber—from the inside out.

What future did Amber face if she didn't receive God's compassion?

What aspect of Amber's story sparks compassionate feelings in you?

How do Amber's acts of compassion impact her own life?

VIBRANT ACTION

Receiving God's Compassion

What would someone discover if they read your autobiography? It may be different than Amber's, but you too have a very personal story. God not only wants to read your life story, but he wants to help you write it.

> Praise be to the God and Father of our Lord Jesus Christ, the Father of compassion and the God of all comfort, who comforts us in all our troubles, so that we can comfort those in any trouble with the comfort we ourselves have received from God. (2 Corinthians 1:3)

God wants a connection to you through his compassionate heart. Think about how God's care for you plays into your life.

Have you ever experienced direct comfort from God in a time of need? How?

Was there ever a circumstance when you felt someone's compassion was a gift from God? When?

In what new way might God be calling you to receive his compassion today? Are you ready to receive it?

Keeping a Close Watch

There are many moments simple and profound when God reaches out to you in compassion. Before you leave your meeting, jot down on a bookmark a quick summary of three times you've received compassion in your life.

During the next two weeks, have the bookmark with you in your wallet, calendar or briefcase. Keep your eyes open for situations where you personally receive God's compassion. Jot these moments down on the bookmark. Ask a friend to check in and ask you what you noticed. Bring your bookmark to the next group meeting. You'll share your reflections then.

TILL WE MEET AGAIN

As you close your time together, pray with your group that

• you'll have eyes to see God's compassion for you

• your heart will be open to a more challenging view of God's compassion

Consider one of the following experiments to do on your own.

• Memorize one of the verses in "God's Autobiography."

• As you watch a newscast or read a newspaper, ask yourself if compassion is a character trait that is valued in society. Why or why not?

Date:_____

Three Times God Showed Me Compassion in the Past

_____

_____

_____

Watching Out for God's Compassion in My Life

Week One

_____

_____

_____

_____

Week Two

_____

_____

_____

_____

Neighbors Close to Me

CHECKING IN WITH GOD: OPENING PRAYER

Invite God to join you as you dive into this learning experience. Pray with your small group that as result of this time together

- God opens your mind to a fresh definition of neighborly compassion
- God brings people to your mind who are in pain or need

OUTRAGEOUS IDEAS

Someone's Dialing 911—Do You Pick Up?

Break out into three groups—A, B and C. Each group should discuss the scenario and the question that follows.

Group A

It's late on a dark, cold winter night. You are walking to your car in the church parking lot. No one is around. A beat up, rusty and dented car pulls up to you. A female person of color is in the car with three children. She asks, "Is the church open? I really need some help. I have nothing to feed my kids tonight, and I don't know what to do." You know the food pantry isn't open at this time. The church staff has left for the day. As you lean toward her to speak with her, you can see that the gas gauge is almost on empty.

What are you thinking and feeling? What do you do?

Group B

Your elderly, widowed neighbor comes home after three months in another state. She was staying with one of her sons after another son died of cancer. You see her taking out her garbage and run over to say hello. She tells you how depressed she is. "I don't feel like doing anything. It's hard to have the energy to eat." You invite her to join your family for dinner one evening. She lists at least three reasons why she cannot come over.

What are you thinking and feeling? What do you do?

Group C

Your brother is getting divorced after twelve years of marriage. His marriage was unstable from the beginning. He is devastated that his family is breaking apart. It's hard for him to have a conversation about anything but his anger, fear, resentment and jealousy. He desperately wants custody of his children. He was also recently laid off at work due to downsizing. He asks for a place to stay and financial support for legal fees.

What are you thinking and feeling? What do you do?

INTENSE INTERIOR

Walking by a 911 Emergency

The story of the good Samaritan is probably one of the most well-known parables in the entire Bible—so well-known that, when we refer to people who do good deeds to others, we say they are "good Samaritans." Close your eyes as the group leader reads the following story.

A religious expert . . . asked Jesus, "Who is my neighbor?"

In reply Jesus said: "A man was going down from Jerusalem to Jericho, when he fell into the hands of robbers. They stripped him of his clothes, beat him and went away, leaving him half dead. A priest happened to be going down the same road, and when he saw the man, he passed by on the other side. So too, a Levite, when he came to the place and saw him, passed by on the other side. But a Samaritan, as he traveled, came where the man was; and when he saw him, he took pity on him. He went to him and bandaged his wounds, pouring on oil and wine. Then he put the man on his donkey, took him to an inn and took care of him. The next day he took out two silver coins and gave them to the innkeeper. 'Look after him,' he said, 'and when I return, I will reimburse you for any extra expense you may have.'

"Which of these three do you think was a neighbor to the man who fell into the hands of the robbers?"

The expert in the law replied, "The one who had mercy on him."

Jesus told him, "Go and do likewise." (Luke 10:25-37)

Continue to keep your eyes closed. Now, imagine this story happened in your neighborhood or nearby urban area. Think about who each character in the story is today. Which character are you?

Now, open your eyes. Share with your group members what you pictured in your mind.

What insights did you get from this reflection exercise?

Compassion and Frustration—Two Sides of One Coin

Read the following, real-life story out loud, with a different group member reading each of the three sections—the beginning, middle and end of the day. Then take a few minutes to discuss the questions that follow.

Beginning. It starts out like any other Sunday. I'm reading the paper and having a cup of coffee. Then the phone rings. It's my brother.

He and his two kids live with my elderly parents. He tells me that my eighty-one-year-old father can't get out of bed. He's dizzy and has been lying in bed for two hours.

I feel helpless and scared. "Have you thought about calling an ambulance?" I ask. "Dad doesn't want me to," my brother replies. I ask, "So, what do you want me to do?" He responds, "He should probably go to a twenty-four-hour immediate care place. But come see for yourself."

When I arrive, my dad is lying in bed, immobile, hesitant to move and act. It's weird to see. We decide to go to the emergency room of a local hospital.

It's 10:30 a.m., and there aren't many people in the small waiting room. But within forty-five minutes, there are at least six patients and their families in the ER. Two of the patients are throwing up into plastic buckets. My mom and brother are very disturbed by this. They're worried we will all catch the flu. We rearrange tables to move away from the coughing and throwing up, but it's a small space; we can't move too far. We wait for two hours.

My brother starts a campaign to leave. "It's worse to stay, because dad can get the flu." My dad turns to me at one point and asks, "What do you think?" I'm flattered that he trusts me, but it's overwhelming to be in this position. What if I suggest the wrong thing? I tell him that if we leave and go to a twenty-four-hour center, they may send him back to the hospital for more extensive tests. We'll waste time. "We may as well wait it out," I said.

Middle. After three hours of waiting, we leave the hospital and move to a twenty-four-hour facility near my parents' home. My mother is increasingly agitated. She is uncomfortable around anyone or anything medical. She is short with the doctor and challenges everything. "Why does my husband need an EKG? He's not complaining about his heart; he's dizzy. Isn't it just an ear infection? Why does he need to go in an ambulance?" The doctor turns to me and asks, "Why is your mom so upset?" I explain that the whole situation is nerve-wracking for her.

Just as I thought: Dad needs more tests. My mother doesn't want this. At 4 p.m. my Dad is escorted in an ambulance back to the hospital we started out at. He waits in the ER another four hours for answers. My family is tense and dad is quiet.

End. When the doctor finally returns with medical results, he starts by apologizing for the delay. He says, "We just lost a fifty-two-year-old man in an urgent situation. I'm sorry you had to wait." I can tell the doctor is affected by this loss. I quickly say, "I'm sorry."

As soon as the doctor leaves, my mom pushes for my dad's IV to be removed and wants my dad to quickly dress. My patience is thin, and it's hard for me to be sympathetic. I emphatically say, "Mom, someone just died, we are not the only ones here. The staff has to take care of that family too." She looks at me—speechless. I wonder what she's thinking. Is she so nervous and scared that she has no consideration for others? How do I help my mom when her behavior is bothering me?

We walk out of the hospital into a cold, dark evening. I take my parents to the store to fill a prescription. The pharmacist tells us, "It will take a half-hour to fill your prescription." I cringe. A half-hour? It's already been an eleven-hour day.

As I enter my house late that evening, numb from the shock of the day, a wave of mixed emotions hits me. My dogs eagerly greet me. I am so grateful my neighbor took care of them today. One less thing to worry about . . .

Who do you most relate to in this scenario?

Who do you think needs compassion in this story?

Who in the story would be the most challenging for you to express compassion toward?

What could you do to take a small compassionate step toward him or her?

23

Vibrant Action

My Compassion Challenge

Do you have a current challenge that is stretching you? Pair up with a person in your group that you don't know well. Take a few minutes to describe your compassion challenge following these prompts:

- Person or people involved: _____
- Situation: _____
- What makes it challenging: _____

Take a few minutes to encourage one another about your challenges, asking what God is calling each of you to do and summarizing what you learned through this discussion. Pray about your compassion challenges together.

Till We Meet Again

As you close your time together, pray with the whole group that

- you will align with God's definition of neighborly compassion
- your heart will open up to opportunities to show compassion to people near you

Consider one of the following experiments on your own.

- Contact your partner between group meetings to discuss your compassion challenge. Share any challenges or breakthroughs that occur. Encourage one another, and commit to praying for one another beyond your group time.

- Watch a movie that illustrates compassionate serving (e.g., *Driving Miss Daisy, I Am Sam, The Bucket List*).

- Label four header boxes "Family," "Friends," "Neighbors" and "Coworkers." In boxes under these headers, list people who have the appropriate connection to you. For each name in the box, note how much you know about their compassion needs (1 = a little, 2 = some, 3 = a lot)

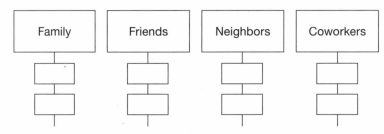

Since the pain of other people isn't always obvious, how might you help each of these people talk about it?

What reluctance do you notice in yourself when it comes to showing compassion to each of these people?

The People Jesus Is Especially Crazy About

CHECKING IN WITH GOD: OPENING PRAYER

As you dive into this learning experience, pray with your small group that as a result of this time together

- God opens your understanding of his special love for marginalized, oppressed and under-resourced people
- God freshly breaks your heart over the things that break his heart

OUTRAGEOUS IDEAS

Just a Train Ride

Imagine you are on a Saturday afternoon train going into the city. You are excited to find a seat where you can sit alone. The train quickly fills up, yet the seat next to you is still open. You come to a stop and see ten people waiting to board the train. They enter your car. The group entering is very diverse. From your line of vision you see a handful of business people, a man and woman with torn and scruffy looking clothes, two teenagers, an elderly woman with a bag, a man of another race, and a mom with a baby.

What are you thinking?

Who do you hope does not sit next to you? Why?

Now, imagine Jesus sitting in the aisle across from you. Who do you think he'd invite to sit next to him? Or who would he move to sit next to? Why?

Stops Along the Way

As we consider Jesus' life, let's take a look at some of Jesus' memories from his travel scrapbook.

> Jesus entered Jericho and was passing through. A man was there by the name of Zacchaeus; he was a chief tax collector and was wealthy. He wanted to see who Jesus was. . . . So he ran ahead and climbed a sycamore-fig tree to see him, since Jesus was coming that way.
>
> When Jesus reached the spot, he looked up and said to him, "Zacchaeus, come down immediately. I must stay at your house today." So he came down at once and welcomed him gladly. All the people saw this and began to mutter, "He has gone to be the guest of a 'sinner.'" (Luke 19:1-8)

> Now he had to go through Samaria. . . . Jacob's well was there, and Jesus, tired as he was from the journey, sat down by the well. . . .
>
> When a Samaritan woman came to draw water, Jesus said to her, "Will you give me a drink?" (His disciples had gone into the town to buy food.)
>
> The Samaritan woman said to him, "You are a Jew and I am a Samaritan woman. How can you ask me for a drink?" (For Jews do not associate with Samaritans.) (John 4:4-9)

> Jesus traveled about from one town and village to another, proclaiming the good news of the kingdom of God. The Twelve were with him, and also some women who had been cured of evil spirits and diseases: Mary (called Magdalene) from whom seven demons had come out; Joanna the wife of Cuza, the manager of Herod's household; Susanna; and many others. (Luke 8:1-3)

Who did Jesus spend time with in these locations?

What kinds of social or relational barriers do you see Jesus moving past with his actions?

How does Jesus' behavior speak to you?

What people in your community are most like the people Jesus hung out with? In our nation? In the world?

INTENSE INTERIOR

Roads to Compassion

We all have different levels of experience, interest and beliefs about the people who are marginalized and oppressed in our society. Our experiences may range from "I am unfamiliar with life situations different than mine" to "I am overwhelmed by the issues certain people face" to "I seek out opportunities to support people who are marginalized."

As we think about the people in our world who are in severe need, we are another step further down the road to becoming crazy enough to care.

As a group, fill out the "Society's Oppressed and Marginalized Worksheet" on page 32, using your response to the final question above. Then have each group member draw a card. You have a maximum of one minute to read, think about and respond as openly as possible to the question on the card. You may "pass" once, but participate at least one time.

Take a few minutes as a group to fill out the "Roadblocks to Compassion" chart (p. 32) with the things that get in the way of your reaching out compassionately to these groups of people. For example, if fear is a roadblock, place the word *fear* in one of the blocks.

VIBRANT ACTION

Delete Fear—Insert Faith

God calls us to remove obstacles on our compassion journey. Jesus offers a clear and radical call to serve the people around us who are in serious need. Read the following silently, or have one group member read it aloud.

Then the King will say to those on his right, "Come, you who are blessed by my Father; take your inheritance, the kingdom prepared for you since the creation of the world. For I was hungry and you gave me something to eat, I was thirsty and you gave me something to drink, I was a stranger and you invited me in, I needed clothes and you clothed me, I was sick and you looked after me, I was in prison and you came to visit me. . . . I tell you the truth, whatever you did for one of the least of these brothers of mine, you did for me." (Matthew 25:34-40)

In spite of this clear call for action, one common, paralyzing concern lifts its ugly head: "With the huge problems in the world, how can I make a difference?"

Jesus has not called us to solve problems; he has commanded us to love people. He isn't asking us to save the world; he is asking us to extend one act of compassion at a time—one cup of cold water, one coat, one hospital visit, one visit to the jailhouse—single actions that show hope to the hurting. Often God infuses these acts with great "replication power."

One Wave Follows Another

Have one group member read the following story out loud.

Alyssa's third grade class heard about the December 2004 tsunami. Being so young, Alyssa didn't have a full grasp of the seriousness of the tragedy, but she understood that families just like hers were now homeless and lost. Alyssa couldn't get the tragedy out of her mind and heart. She talked about it with her grandmother and mother.

Alyssa called her relatives and asked for pledges if she read a certain number of hours a week. Her goal was to earn $150 in pledges, which she would, in turn, donate to the tsunami victims. Her parents joined her enthusiasm. Alyssa's mom called her friend's mother. That phone call led to another family joining in, and so on and so on. Soon Alyssa's entire third grade was participating in a tsunami read-a-thon at school. Forty-two children came to the school gym to read.

The kids raised almost $5,000—the amount was beyond any-one's expectations. The parents, teachers and local community were touched by the passion and action Alyssa and her friends took. The kids understood what they were doing for the people of Indonesia and why. After the read-a-thon, Alyssa asked her mom, "Mom, do you think that if we do 'Read 4 Relief' until I'm a mom there won't be any hungry people in the world anymore?"

What do you notice about Alyssa's response to this tragedy?

What do you think triggered Alyssa's innocent, compassionate response?

How can we be more like Alyssa as we consider compassionate acts?

TILL WE MEET AGAIN

The next session in this adventure is a group serving opportunity. As you close your time together, pray that

- you grasp God's vast love toward people in serious need and his replication power made available to us as we step up to serve

- you prepare your mind, heart and hands for your upcoming serving opportunity

Consider one of the following experiments on your own.

- Watch a movie that highlights compassionate acts across all kinds of barriers: racial, ethnic, social, socioeconomic. A couple movies to consider are *Pay It Forward* and *Radio*.

- Journal about a serving opportunity in your life that has potential for the kind of multiplication that Alyssa's read-a-thon generated.

Roads to Compassion Activity, Part 1
Society's Oppressed and Marginalized Worksheet

Note: The boxes on this worksheet are to be filled in with descriptions of people who are most oppressed and marginalized in our society.

	R	O	A	D	S
1	R1	O1	A1	D1	S1
2	R2	O2	A2	D2	S2
3	R3	O3	A3	D3	S3
4	R4	O4	A4	D4	S4
5	R5	O5	A5	D5	S5

Roadblocks to Compassion

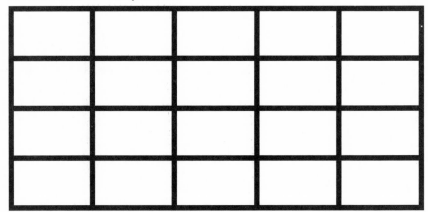

Extending My Hands

group serving experience gives you an opportunity to encounter compassion firsthand. By proactively assisting people in need, you become the hands and feet of Jesus to the people you serve. In serving you receive as much as, if not more than, you give. Serving is a powerful way to experience God.

Serving opportunities can focus on

- family or friends in need
- people from your church
- your local community
- nearby under-resourced, urban areas
- ministries involved in compassionate community service

Options to extend compassionate hands are as endless as the number of grains of sand. Here are a few ideas to get your mental juices flowing:

- visiting the elderly
- providing lawn or home maintenance care to the sick or homebound
- visiting a nursing home or hospital
- providing home or auto repair to a single parent
- delivering resources to local refugees
- coordinating meals for a homeless shelter
- collecting food in your neighborhood for the under-resourced
- delivering meals to the sick and infirmed

It is beneficial to set aside time after your serving experience to discuss its impact on you and your team members.

What was it like interacting with people as you served?

What did you learn the most?

How did you experience Jesus in the moment?

5

Relationships That Reflect God's Compassion

CHECKING IN WITH GOD: OPENING PRAYER

As you dive into this learning experience, pray with your small group that as a result of this time together

- God uses this real-life story to prompt you to think about people in your life who are in similar need

- God reveals to you how the power of the Holy Spirit can shine through you

OUTRAGEOUS IDEAS

This session is entirely focused on the intense interior experience of being consistently compassionate. Have a group member read the following story out loud, then discuss the questions that follow.

A Friendship in Need

Nona and Barbara's friendship began at a young age. In their mid-twenties, Barbara and Nona became especially close as they were thrown into similar life circumstances. Both divorced early in life, they bonded and became dependent on one another for support and encouragement.

Thirty years into the friendship, earth-shaking news changed their lives. Through tests taken because of a lingering cold, Barbara learned that she had an aggressive form of breast cancer. In her late forties, she was given thirty days to live. She was single, without a supportive family, financially drained and emotionally devastated.

Nona wasn't going to let Barbara go through this alone. Once a week, she took Barbara for chemo treatments. "It was important for Barbara to have some independence. This time was not only emotionally difficult for her, but financially difficult. She was in a time of financial hardship and was very private about her situation. Her dying wish was to live in her own home. My sister, also a friend of Barbara's, helped fund a home for her." Barbara was put on a trial chemotherapy drug which extended her life. But, after a reprieve, the cancer returned and this time moved into her lungs. Nona and a small handful of friends supported Barbara.

Although the person receiving needed care, Barbara also carried a big concern: "How is Nona going to survive this?" Nona was "running around like crazy" and feeling "stretched limb to limb." Caring for both her family and Barbara felt like "an emotional tug of war." Barbara knew that Nona was carrying a lot and was concerned for her.

What might it be like to suddenly become so dependent on others?

Imagine that you are in Nona's position. What would you be willing to give up or change to accommodate the significant needs of a loved one or friend?

How do you hope your friends would respond if you suddenly found yourself in physical and financial need?

Intense interior

A Neighbor—Becoming a New Friend

Read the next passage silently, then discuss in pairs your responses to the questions that follow it.

Pat, one of Nona's neighbors, had met Barbara a handful of times over the years. She knew that Nona was Barbara's primary caregiver. A serving coordinator for her neighborhood church group, Pat had a heart for the total well-being of people in her neighborhood. Pat could deliver help because she was a member of two small groups that were looking for opportunities to serve people in need.

One winter day, standing in Nona's driveway, Pat asked Nona if Barbara was willing to accept help from others or interested in talking with a pastor. Not wanting to make the decision for her, Nona presented the idea to Barbara. When Barbara said OK, Pat contacted her and set up a time to meet. Pat invited Sue, a community pastor, to join the first meeting with them.

The day of the first meeting arrived. When the doorbell rang, Barbara, out of breath, opened the door to Pat, an acquaintance, and Sue, a stranger. Barbara was open to these women because she trusted Nona

The goal of the first conversation was to help Barbara feel comfortable with assistance. Pat and Sue could tell that this meeting was physically and emotionally difficult for Barbara. She had trouble breathing even on oxygen. Pat and Sue expressed their sincere concern for Barbara and her well-being, and then respectfully offered suggestions about how they might assist her.

Beyond caring about her physical wellness, Pat and Sue wanted to express concern for the wellness of her soul too. Sue gently asked Barbara, "Do you know where you are going after you die?" Barbara responded, "I hope to heaven." Sue then explained that Barbara could receive God's gift of grace and eternal salvation through Christ's death on the cross. She could have the peace of knowing for sure.

When they left at the end of their visit, not only was Barbara left with a new plan for how her physical needs could be helped, but she also had a lot to ponder spiritually.

Is it easier for you to attend to someone's physical or spiritual needs? Why?

If you were Barbara, what would have been the most uncomfortable aspect of this encounter for you?

What kinds of things are important relationally when approaching a person in need? How did Pat and Sue model this?

A Friendship Circle Grows

Join up with other pairs so that your whole group is split in half. Take a few minutes to silently read the section below; then discuss the questions that follow in your group.

Upon returning home, Pat immediately emailed one of her small-group members, Patrick, who in turn quickly contacted others in the group to set a date for the group to serve Barbara. On a cold Saturday morning, six men showed up at Barbara's house. Some of the men knew the severity of her illness, but they all knew that she needed assistance and were eager to help.

Over the next two months, various people did items on her "honey do" list—mostly small tasks such as shoveling snow, picking up medicine, repairing little things around the house, shopping for groceries and moving furniture. Group members were excited to have this chance to be Jesus' hands and feet in Barbara's life.

Their service really touched Barbara and those people around her. Barbara began to trust the people serving her and began to ask other people who were serving her about their faith. Pat began to take Barbara to doctor appointments. During these car rides, the conversation often turned spiritual. Barbara talked with Pat about things like prayer, grief over unfulfilled dreams and dependence on God for wisdom in her circumstance.

Although Nona was like a sister to her, "faith topics were hard for us to talk about. Barbara was reserved about her faith," says Nona. "I think she avoided discussions because if she talked about it, she thought that she would die. She was insecure and afraid about where she stood spiritually. Sue and the team really got to Barbara.

I am relieved that Sue comforted Barbara in a way that I couldn't."

As the weeks passed, Barbara was repeatedly amazed by the continual support of these people. A financial fund was pooled to contribute to her needs. Barbara shared with Sue that, "prior to my illness, I thought I was a Christian. But experiencing this team's love toward me, I realize I wasn't."

Why do you think serving someone's physical needs can open the door to spiritual conversations?

VIBRANT ACTION

Contagious Compassion Impacts Long-Term Serving

Rejoin the group as a whole and have one group member read the remaining part of the story out loud. Then discuss the questions that follow.

During the time that the group served Barbara, she made the decision to receive God's peace for her life, trusting Christ for her ultimate salvation and spiritual healing. Shortly after she made this decision, Barbara died.

Sue had talked to Barbara about a funeral that would celebrate her life. Barbara agreed to the celebration concept, but she didn't have a church she called home. While never having stepped in the building, Barbara chose to have her funeral at her serving team's church.

Until the funeral, the serving team hadn't realized the full impact of their service. Barbara had told everyone about them. She was amazed and uncomfortable that all these people wanted to help her. "How can I ever repay their kindness?" Many friends and family members attended the funeral and heard the amazing story of Barbara's final days.

Conversations sprang up in the community about how and why the group was serving Barbara. "The walls have come down in our community," Patrick observes. "People are ready and interested in hearing why we served someone like Barbara, why we want to be the hands and feet of Jesus to our neighbors."

The story of compassion for Barbara even became a discussion item at Village Hall. The village government heard about the group and connected the group to an older couple who needed help with lawn care because the husband had a brain injury.

"Our small group evolved by serving Barbara," says Patrick. Nona reflects, "I was pulled in two directions between caring for my family and Barbara. I didn't realize how hard it was until I stopped doing it. But I couldn't always be there for my friend. I am so appreciative for the serving team. I am grateful for Pat and the day she approached me in my driveway."

How are people in Barbara's situation—single, divorced, ill and financially under-resourced—typically treated by society?

Barbara's serving team was crazy enough to step out of their comfort zones and serve Barbara. Would you be truly willing and available to do the same? Why or why not?

TILL WE MEET AGAIN

As you close your time together, pray that

- God will give you new insight on how one act of compassion replicates
- your confidence increases in the role God wants you to play in his plan to show compassion to a hurting world

Consider one of the following experiments on your own.

- Between now and the next session, write a one-minute, five-minute and fifteen-minute version of your story of faith. What has been your journey? What were marking moments in your spiritual development?

How would you explain your journey to a non-Christian?

- Read a book on evangelism, such as *Becoming a Contagious Christian* by Bill Hybels and Mark Mittelberg or *Just Walk Across the Room* by Bill Hybels.

God's Love for Variety

6

Checking in with God: Opening Prayer

As you dive into this learning experience, pray with your small group that as a result of this time together

- you freshly see how people prejudge one another and separate by race

- God shows you his desire for respect and reconciliation among all races, especially among Christians

Outrageous Ideas

A Hidden Camera

Read the following setting together as a group, with one group member serving as narrator and two group members playing the specific characters. Discuss the questions that follow.

> *Scene: bakery in Chicago, Illinois.* Narrator: It's a cold, blustery morning on the North Side of Chicago. The streets are busy with people racing in and out of drug stores, banks and coffee stands. The best bakery in town has a line out the front door of a wide variety of customers from all races and income levels. At the front of the line is Sabina, an Islamic woman. She is wearing a jihab, or head scarf. She's heard about the excellent desserts at this bakery. Getting up early to be one of the first people in line, she has been waiting thirty minutes for the store to open. She is preparing for a family celebration and wants to buy special pastries for the event.

Sabina: "Good morning. You have so many delicious pastries to choose from."

Cashier: (No response, looks at her then, looks past her to the next person in line.)

Sabina: "I will take two cinnamon coffee cakes please."

Cashier: (Just stares at her.)

Sabina: "Excuse me. I will take two cinnamon coffee cakes please."

Cashier: (Stares at her, then looks past her and says "Next" to the person behind her.)

Sabina: "I'm sorry; I must not be speaking loud enough. I'd like two cinnamon coffee cakes please."

Cashier: "I heard you. We don't serve your kind here."

Sabina: "Pardon me?"

Cashier: "Get back on your camel, and go back to where you came from."

Narrator: Sabina looks distressed. Her eyes filling with tears, she turns to the person behind her.

Sabina: "Would you please order my coffee cakes for me?"

Suppose you're the customer behind Sabina. What are you thinking and feeling?

How would you respond to Sabina?

For the person reading Sabina's lines, how did it feel to have another person treat you this way? What is your immediate response?

This scene actually occurred as a social experiment by *ABC Primetime News.* The Muslim woman received these responses from people in line when she asked for help:

- Some customers actually supported the owner's rude and offensive behavior; the Muslim woman left the store.

- Some customers passionately defended the Muslim woman and argued with the owner about his act of discrimination.

- A majority of people did nothing. They looked the other way and did not look the Muslim woman in the eye.

Which of these three responses do you think is the most dangerous? Why?

Read the following quotations from Jesus and his followers.

"Love the Lord your God with all your heart and with all your soul and with all your mind." This is the first and greatest commandment. And the second is like it: "Love your neighbor as yourself." All the Law and the Prophets hang on these two commandments. (Matthew 22:37-40)

My brothers and sisters, as believers in our glorious Lord Jesus Christ, don't show favoritism. (James 2:1)

There before me was a great multitude that no one could count, from every nation, tribe, people and language, standing before the throne and in front of the Lamb. (Revelation 7:9)

If Jesus was standing behind Sabina, what would he do?

INTENSE INTERIOR

Rewinding the Tape

Take time to answer the following questions individually, in private.

How would I really react to the Muslim woman in the bakery if she asked for my help? What would I say to her? The cashier?

If my friend of another race was insulted verbally in a store, would I defend him or her? Why or why not?

What are my assumptions—general and specific—about people of other races?

What makes me uncomfortable interacting with other races?

Have I ever been the victim of wrongdoing by a person of another race?

How might the experience have affected my thoughts and feelings about his or her race?

Where would I place myself on the following continuum of race relations?

☐ **Deny:** I don't believe there's a problem when it comes to race in our society. There's nothing I or society needs to do differently to promote equality among races.

☐ **Know:** I know about and understand racial reconciliation issues. I am exploring how I and society can promote equality among races.

☐ **Challenge:** I am challenging my Christian worldview regarding racial reconciliation. I am getting involved in promoting equality among races.

☐ **Participate:** I proactively participate in matters related to racial reconciliation.

Vibrant Action

It is good to come before God and confess that we have been exclusive and separatist in our attitudes and behavior. Pray as a group, acknowledging to God that race matters in our society and that race matters to you. God has an opposite plan for us—that, as members of the body of Christ, we are one. Allow some space for silent prayer as a group, using prompts provided by your leader.

Till We Meet Again

Consider one of the following experiments on your own.

- Watch the movie *In My Country,* with Samuel L. Jackson.
- Journal your observations as to how God is guiding you through the Scripture passages discussed during this session.

7

God's Call to Cross the Divide

CHECKING IN WITH GOD: OPENING PRAYER

As you dive into this learning experience, pray with your small group that as a result of this time together

- you freshly understand God's expectations about racial inclusivity and what this means for unity in the body of Christ

- the Holy Spirit prompts you to reach out across all types of racial divides, even if it causes discomfort or fear

OUTRAGEOUS IDEAS

Gracious Moments of Truth

Did you know that one of the most beautiful and best-loved Christian songs was born out of a grief-stricken heart? "Amazing Grace," written by John Newton in 1772, is a response to his awakening sense of wrongdoing, shame and guilt. He led a ship that took Africans from their home during the slave trade. This song is a testimony about Newton finding salvation in Christ during a ferocious storm that killed many people on his slave ship.

Only God's power can take a broken and hardened heart and create the humble spirit reflected in the song "Amazing Grace." It has deep personal meaning to millions of people around the world and is a favorite song among supporters of freedom and human rights. The following stories also tell of personal pain, reflection and change in the area of extending grace to others. Break into four groups to read and discuss one of the following true stories about racial reconciliation.

Story one: one minute away from expulsion. I am originally from India; I grew up around Hindus and Muslims and Sikhs and all kinds of different religions. All my neighbors were mixed races. I didn't have a challenge until I came to the United States. In 1974, when I was in a Bible College in Atlanta, Georgia, I started liking a certain young lady, Brenda, who was from Michigan. We both worked on campus as students—me a janitor, and she a secretary to the dean's office.

Brenda is white and I am not. This fact caused a real upheaval on campus, especially among the board and administration. The board got together and ruled that no one could date anyone outside their own ethnic background. They defined *dating* as any conversation over a minute.

On three different occasions, the dean threatened to expel me because of my relationship with Brenda. When you are a foreign student and you get expelled, you are deported. Once you're deported, that's the end of ever coming back to the country. Brenda and I couldn't sit in class together, sit in the same church pew, eat together or drive in a car together. So we made cassette tapes for one another and had people pass notes for us; we still have those notes in boxes in our attic.

In 1979, Brenda and I decided to get married. The campus was in turmoil. Our campus pastor said he wouldn't marry us because he didn't feel it was the "right thing and it couldn't work." It was known that if I married Brenda, I would not be welcome in our church anymore. Brenda was told that if she married me, she would go to hell. We went through all kind of inner turmoil. After we got married, we packed up and moved to Oregon, to put some distance immediately between us and the college community. Later we moved to Michigan, where I became pastor of a local church.

Fast forward. Brenda and I have been married twenty-nine years. Every one of the school's board members, one at a time, has apologized to me. Neither my wife nor I held resentment. It was not in my nature or Brenda's nature to strike back. There was nothing to gain. I know hurt people tend to hurt other people. I kept relationships with the board members from Atlanta. I invited some of them to come speak at my church; some even spent the night in our Michigan home.

Years later, I came back to this very college to become its president. The reason I believe God brought me back to the college was twofold. First, for the institution itself, because we saw phenomenal multiracial growth. More than that, the Lord brought me back so that I could face my own demons. Across the hall from me was the man who threatened me with expulsion. Some of the same board members were still there. I had to interact with them on a professional, personal and Christian level. It was a choice I made to come back. Healing was a process.

I see that racial bigotry is not a rational issue; it's an emotional issue. It is something amorphous, ambiguous, vague . . . just floating somewhere inside of a person. Because it's not rational, you can't really talk and discuss it out. This is why, when I became president of the college, I had zero tolerance for bigotry and racism. In some cases, I had to let racist staff go. Someone has got to break the cycle. (Dr. Samuel Chand)

What are your general reactions to the story?

Was racial reconciliation achieved? Why or why not?

What made reconciliation possible?

Story two: wounds that go deep. As a black man, some of my earliest memories are of cruel comments and horrendous behavior. When I was about five or six years old, a white man came up to me and thumped me on the head and said, "Boy, who are you the daddy of?" I told him my dad's name. "Boy, you ain't old enough to be nobody's daddy!" Another time, I was with my cousin, and a boy came toward us with a B-B gun and said, "I'm going to shoot you niggers." I knew at a young age that I couldn't fight back because the boy was white. I remember thinking, *It won't hurt much.*

Humiliation became a theme in my life and in the lives of the people I loved. You feel so helpless in the face of humiliation. My greatest grief was when my brother was killed at age sixteen by a police officer. He was in line in an ally, waiting to get into a theater with his girlfriend. A group of kids were laughing and having a good time. A policeman, wanting the crowd to be quiet, came over and hit my brother in the head with a leather club. My brother turned around to reach for the club and the policeman pulled out a gun and shot him. They wouldn't take my brother at the local doctor's office, so we had to drive fifty miles to a hospital in Jackson, Mississippi. When we arrived there, he was dead. Hours and moments of my memory after he was killed are lost.

It was after that time that I began to think about leaving Mississippi. I moved to California. My white friends there helped me process the pain I felt. I actively became a leader during the Civil Rights period in the United States. Deciding to "make peace," I returned to Mississippi. There, because of my stand for civil rights, I was jailed and tortured. A few of us had gone to the jailhouse in Brandon, Mississippi, to talk to the sheriff about releasing African American students who were arrested for no reason. Instead of the sheriff coming out to talk to us, several highway patrolmen came out of the building, searched us and arrested us. We were beaten almost to the point of death. I tried to cover my head with my arms, but they just beat me anyway until I was lying on the floor. I was kicked in the head, in the ribs, in the groin. I was in and out of consciousness. A bent fork was pushed in my nose and down my throat. Even though I was in a stupor, they made me work at mopping up my own blood.

The sin of my torturers—hatred—was passed on to me. My faith in Christ told me to forgive, but for a long time, I pushed this thought in the background and felt justified for my hatred. Over the next couple of years I struggled with serious health issues while appeals were made on the charges against me in the Brandon arrest. I was wrestling with the feeling that there was no justice, no hope.

I began to see with horror how hate could destroy me. But in the pain, there was healing taking place. God was showing me something. Hope was restored as I realized that change was happening.

It wasn't until an old white policeman came to me that reconciliation came to me fully. I put up a tent to preach against crime. This policeman came and thought the tent event was wonderful. He kept moving toward me. It was our common vision and mission for our community that helped us see one another with love.

Reconciliation didn't happen in a church "house" for me. This particular old man helped me get a filling of the spirit of reconciliation. His willingness to see people different than himself motivated me to reconcile. I saw that both blacks and whites believe in justice.

The image of the cross blotted out everything else in my mind. Jesus knew what I had suffered. He experienced it all himself. When Jesus looked at the mob that lynched him, he didn't hate them. He loved them. He forgave them. His enemies hated. But Jesus forgave. I couldn't get away from that. (Dr. John Perkins)

What are your general reactions to the story?

Was racial reconciliation achieved? Why or why not?

What made reconciliation possible?

Story three: a long walk. I was born in Texas; my parents were born in Texas. One of my grandparents is from Texas. So we're Americans of Mexican descent. When I was young, six or seven years old, my grandfather would take me for long walks into Mexico. He would always say to me that I had to be careful of the Anglo person. He'd say, "You're gonna be living with these folks and they'll take advantage of you. You're gonna have to stand up for yourself and you're gonna have to watch out." Here's my granddad, who I look up to and adore, and he's telling me this.

I lived through the whole Jim Crow segregation—which, a lot of times, we think was focused on African Americans. But in Texas there were bathrooms that said, "Whites only, no Mexicans allowed."

When I was still young my family moved to California. Spanish was my first language, and I wound up at an all white school. There were not very many Latinos in California at that time. Everyday, I would get chased home and beat up on the way to school by white kids. They wanted to beat up on the Spanish speaking kids that "couldn't talk right." I knew I was being treated differently because of the color of my skin, because of my race.

As a sophomore in high school, I got involved with Young Life through my football coach, a white dude from Stanford University. He did a great job of getting us guys to camp and loving us. Two things impacted me at camp: First, I learned that Jesus will change my life forever. I never knew Jesus loved me or that he came to this earth in person. The second thing that really impacted me was that, out of three hundred kids at this camp, there were only five kids of color. I wondered, *Does Jesus speak for everybody—or is it just for white kids?* I was a Christian only a couple of days thinking these thoughts.

As time passed, I joined the Young Life Staff in San Francisco. I was excited to work with Latino kids, but my first assignment as a staff person was with twelve Chinese kids in Chinatown! I was thinking, *I don't wanna go. I don't know anything about Chinese kids, and I have no desire to do this at all.* By the end of the week I was just loving these kids. We were doing kung fu—exercising every morning, hanging out and wrestling. They just loved me. They included me, and I learned about them and their culture. That showed me how sometimes God has to put us into situations to stretch us because, left to our own devices, we'd stay to ourselves.

Sometimes, it feels like the bridge or the gap between cultures is so huge. It feels too hard to cross. That's my honest feeling sometimes. Yet I think that when God's Spirit is in us, we have this ability. When we can look at people the way God looks at people and love them for who they are. (Noel Castellanos)

What are your general reactions to the story?

Was racial reconciliation achieved? Why or why not?

What made reconciliation possible?

Story four: unexpected learning. Racial reconciliation is important in my ministry. There are times I need to travel down paths with others that, as a white guy, I don't necessarily understand.

During one season of ministry, I was serving with an African American friend, David. I was already having interactions with him because our roles crossed in ministry. Our relationship started completely unrelated to the pursuit of racial reconciliation. As our relationship and friendship matured, the topic of racial reconciliation became more important—because it was important to him.

Having a friend of another race became a process of discovery. I mean, my background is one where I don't quite understand why everything is such a big deal for minorities. It wasn't a "recognition of injustice" that necessarily prompted me to pursue racial reconciliation. I had to recognize things in my own life, more than any grand social cause.

When I looked at my beliefs in younger years, I wasn't actively racist, but I didn't necessarily grow up with favorable impressions of other races either. Some of the stereotypes had negative associations. There wasn't hatred; it was a much more Christian version. When David and I became friends, my perspective about the importance of race shifted. I now do not become tired of talking about race, because I have a friend, and many other friends, whose lives are impacted by racial issues. I care about these friends. I care about what they care about.

I learned a lot from David. For example, imagine being nine years old and realizing that for the rest of your life, while probably not being in danger of physical harm, five out of six people will not give you the benefit of the doubt, will begin interacting with you not because they want to but because they have to, and generally prefer that you keep out of their lives. I think African Americans live in just such a world. I think the people who created such an unfriendly place for blacks to live in were people like me: nonviolent, church-going, family people. I created in my mind certain stereotypes about blacks, and I let these stereotypes permeate my thoughts, my words, my heart and my relationships. I generally just didn't like black people, and I preferred that my life not interact with too many on a personal level.

The more David and I talked about race, I realize that although I had not been overtly racist, I had been passively racist, and I asked for his forgiveness. I continue to grow in understanding. What I learn in one setting can be applied to other settings. Some of the things that I can learn from David, about African Americans, can be applied to my employees and peers who are Asian, Middle Eastern or Hispanic. Each racial group has different cultural dynamics, and each person has different life perspectives. But I never stop learning, and I always have to make sure that God is the focus and I am not. (Brent Zuercher)

What are your general reactions to the story?

Was racial reconciliation achieved? Why or why not?

What made reconciliation possible?

What Makes Reconciliation Work?

Bring the whole group back together. Have each group report on their discussion, summarizing each reconciliation story and identifying one or two takeaways about the reconciliation process.

There's a pattern to the reconciliation process.

Inquiry: Openness; willingness to listen and learn from different perspectives; willingness to receive feedback about how behaviors affect others

Awareness: Understanding; ability to see and appreciate different perspectives; ability to acknowledge how behaviors affect others

Repentance: Admitting negative attitudes and behaviors and how they affect other people; turning away from negative attitudes and behaviors and replacing them with positive ones

Where have you seen this reconciliation pattern in your own life?

How could you apply this pattern to opportunities for racial reconciliation in your life?

Intense interior

Crossing the Divide of Fear and Distrust
Divide up so each person has his or her own space. Craft a letter using the following outline.

Dear God,

After our discussion about amazing grace and racial reconciliation I feel:

If I were to write a letter across a racial divide, it would be addressed to:

What I really want to say to this person is:

What I really want to ask this person is:

What I hope to hear is:

What I'd like to tell this person that I feel badly about:

What I'd like to change in my attitudes or behavior is:

I could use this person's help crossing the divide, if he or she would:

My ultimate desire in this relationship is:

With heartfelt sincerity,

VIBRANT ACTION

One Prayer Closer to Unity
Close as a group in a time of guided healing prayer, modeled after the move away from isolation and separation toward unity.

TILL WE MEET AGAIN

Consider one of the following experiments on your own.

- Watch the movie *Glory Road, Remember the Titans* or *Akeelah and the Bee.*
- Consider steps you could take toward racial reconciliation.

Inquiry

- Pray that God would give you the desire to pursue racial reconciliation.
- Seek out relationships with people of different races.

Awareness

- Read books, watch movies, listen to radio programs to learn about race issues from different racial perspectives.
- Develop a friendship with someone of another race, and listen to how race matters in his or her life.

Repentance

- Acknowledge to yourself, God and others you trust any negative attitudes and behaviors toward other races, and commit to turning away from your negative attitudes and behaviors.
- Actively pursue racial reconciliation with someone of another race.

Exploring Justice for All

CHECKING IN WITH GOD: OPENING PRAYER

As you dive into this learning experience, pray with your small group that as a result of this time together

- God grows your understanding of what justice is and why it is important to him
- God gives you fresh thinking and clarity on why this topic is important to people today

OUTRAGEOUS IDEAS

At the Tip of My Tongue

Check off the words below that you immediately associate with the word *justice.*

Judgment	Persistence	Fair	Love
Happiness	Concern	Gift	Freedom
Disappointment	Impossible	Revenge	Unfair
Peace	Glorious	Unreal	Sacrifice
Vengeance	Satisfaction	Support	Patience
Persuasive	Truth	Payment	Consequence
Equal	Perseverance	Frustration	Expensive
Righteous	Compassion	Accountability	Punishment
Retribution	Legal	Inclusive	Difficult

Jesus—the Ultimate Advocate

Scholars, politicians, rulers, "average Joes and Joans"—people through-out history have debated whether or not God shows favor to certain peo-ple. Well, he does. Are you shocked to know this? Maybe you are aware of this fact but haven't thought about it recently. Jesus was clear about who is on his priority list:

> The Spirit of the Lord is on me, because he has anointed me to preach good news to the poor. He has sent me to proclaim freedom for the prisoners and recovery of sight for the blind, to release the oppressed, to proclaim the year of the Lord's favor. (Luke 4:18-19)

Jesus' heart beats fast for the weak and outcast. As the strong one, he rescues people whom others pity, oppress, victimize and torture.

Jesus is our advocate for just and fair treatment. He had harsh words for the religious leaders of his day who walked with heads held high:

> Woe to you, teachers of the law and Pharisees, you hypocrites! You give a tenth of your spices—mint, dill and cumin. But you have ne-glected the more important matters of the law—justice, mercy and faithfulness. (Matthew 23:23)

Revelation about Jesus' priorities begins in the Old Testament. God shares with the prophet Isaiah that Jesus is "my servant, whom I uphold, my chosen one in whom I delight; I will put my Spirit on him and he will bring justice to the nations" (Isaiah 42:1).

Why does God seek justice for the oppressed?

What other people, not referred to here, does God advocate for?

When Saying "I'm Sorry" Isn't Enough

Each one of us makes mistakes. Whatever role we have in life, our poor choices impact people around us: a few people or hundreds or even thousands. Consider the story of Marion Jones.

In 2000 she became the first woman to win five medals at one Olympics, including three gold medals in track and field. By 2003 she was under investigation for using performance-enhancing drugs. She claimed she did not.

Then in 2006, Marion tested positive for the performance-enhancing drug erythropoietin (EPO). She pled guilty to federal charges for using a steroid known as "the clear." She told family and friends that her former coach gave her the drug and she didn't know what it was. She was told it was flaxseed oil. Marion confessed to making false statements during different government investigations.

Marion had to forfeit all race results since September 2000 and return all her medals and money, including the $700,000 prize money. In her prime, Marion was earning between $70,000 and $80,000 a race, plus at least another $1 million from bonuses and endorsement deals. A prison sentence was also a consequence of her actions.

According to the *Washington Post,* Marion said to family and friends, "I want to apologize for all of this. I am sorry for disappointing you all in so many ways."

If you were one of Marion's competitors, having trained for many years, would an apology be enough for you to correct the damages in this situation? Why or why not?

Do you think Marion's consequences were fair or harsh? Why?

Intense interior

Justice or Not

Discuss as a group each person's personal experience as related to justice, using the sentence-starter cards as a guide. (See p. 137.)

How did you feel when this situation happened to you?

How did you cope with the situation?

Was justice served to the person wronged? If not, why?

Vibrant action

Have one person read the following poem (by Marie Guthrie) twice, pausing for a few moments after each sentence. Dwell privately on the implications of this situation for a couple minutes; then discuss the questions that follow as a group.

Shocking Penalty

I did it.
I tried to stop myself.
I tried to talk myself out of it.
It was too tempting—energy, power, control.
Anger burning.
I am right. They are wrong.
I weakened.
I did it.
Now, I stand.
In front of the judge.
Waiting.
No more control.
Stern looks.
Glances of disgust.
To my right.

One.
One alone.
Pleads my case.
Pleads for mercy.

"No mercy today," says the gavel.

Justice today.

Life sentence.

No appeal.

No parole—ever.

Forever.

Same one.

One to my right.

Stands up.

Moves forward.

Approaches judge.

Says, "Me instead."

Gasp.

Shock.

Disbelief.

Anger.

"Fool!" the room cries.

One.

One turns to me.

Says . . .

"Believe it."

Eyes down.

Hands forward.

Taken away.

Gavel pounds.

"Case closed."

Justice served.

Court adjourned.

One.

Left envelope.

Hands shaking.

Open.

Invoice.

Stamp mark "Paid in Full."

I am free.

Free.

Have someone in your group read these verses:

For God so loved the world that he gave his one and only Son, that whoever believes in him shall not perish but have eternal life. For God did not send his Son into the world to condemn the world, but to save the world through him. Whoever believes in him is not condemned, but whoever does not believe stands condemned already because he has not believed in the name of God's one and only son. (John 3:16-18)

Talk about a time you did something wrong and didn't get what you deserved. Who absorbed the consequence of your actions?

Through Jesus' death on the cross, he absorbed God's justice and took away the eternal consequences of your sin.

God presented him as a sacrifice of atonement, through faith in his blood. He did this to demonstrate his justice, because in his forbearance he had left the sins committed beforehand unpunished. (Romans 3:25)

What does God want you to do with this information?

How can you act on it?

TILL WE MEET AGAIN

Close your time as a group in prayer, asking God to help you

- understand the role of justice in God's heavenly court room
- act on the news that God absorbed the consequences for your wrongdoings and removed your eternal sentence apart from him with a gift of freedom

Consider one of the following experiments on your own.

- Between now and the next session, take some time to dwell on how

Jesus' death was a payment for your wrongdoings and mistakes. In what sense is Jesus' death all about justice?

- Share your thoughts and feelings about God's justice with a friend or confidant.

A Radical Righter of Wrongs

Am I One?

CHECKING IN WITH GOD: OPENING PRAYER

As you dive into this learning experience, pray with your small group that as a result of this time together

- God opens your eyes to the fact that people are consistently cheated, ripped off, abandoned and betrayed
- God opens your eyes to the fact that he seeks restoration for people taken advantage of

OUTRAGEOUS IDEAS

Happily Ever After—NOT

Have different members of the group read each of the stories below, and discuss the questions listed.

Story one: favor causes jealousy. Since fifth grade, because of his extreme helpfulness to his teachers, Connor was called TP—teacher's pet. In the seventh grade, for example, Connor made friends with a handicapped boy and wheeled him back and forth from class to lunch every day. It was common for Connor to be recognized at student appreciation assemblies. A group of boys in his class made fun of him, but they were actually very jealous. In high school, Connor's natural likeability landed him a shot at homecoming king.

On the day of student voting, the candidates for homecoming

king agreed to play a prank on one of the girls up for queen. When her name was called, the guys turned their back on her and dropped their pants. Connor, however, refused and walked off stage. The school administration was so impressed with his integrity they named him homecoming king.

The guys, feeling betrayed by Connor, burned with anger. They plotted to ruin Connor's reputation. The week after homecoming, they broke into Connor's locker and placed marijuana in it. Through a "tip," the local police were alerted to a drug problem in the school. After the dogs sniffed down his locker, Connor was escorted to the principal's office. A day later, he was sent to a juvenile detention center for three weeks, despite the protest of family and his family's lawyer. There he received two beatings from other teenagers, resulting in a broken hand. He was finally acquitted only to never be able to play his favorite game of tennis in high school again.

What shocks you the most about this story? Why?

Was justice served in this story? If not, what would justice look like?

Story two: let my employees go. Employees of an aerosol spray company started to complain of severe headaches. When approached by the plant manager, the company president blamed a new air compression machine, loud with a high-pitched ring, for the headaches. The president ordered earmuffs and plugs for the 150 employees.

When one of the employees had a seizure, the plant manager begged the president to act. He wouldn't. The factory was non-union, so there was no one to represent the workers. Living in a financially depressed town, the workers couldn't hire a lawyer, and if they quit, there were no other jobs in the community. The employees had only two options. Either they quit their jobs and go hungry or stay at the plant and risk exposure to continued health trauma.

When two employees died of seizures on the same day, the plant manager staged an all-employee walkout. Regional media caught wind of the tragedy and began an investigation. The president, whose reputation was in question, turned the tables and attempted to sue employees for breaking their contracts.

What shocks you the most about this story? Why?

Was justice served in this story? If not, what would justice look like?

Story three: don't look back. The island was avoided by the rest of the world. Although beautiful, it suffered an HIV/AIDS epidemic. Only occasionally would someone from the mainland, typically a doctor, come to give medicine to the islanders.

A group of islanders were digging a trench for water when they saw a sparkling red glow. They thought it was the sun playing tricks on their eyes, but after continuing to dig, they unearthed an underground cave. Along the cave's perimeter were gems never seen before—a hybrid between a ruby and diamond.

This discovery quickly became news. Wealthy people competed with one another to buy a piece of the island from the local government. People with HIV/AIDS were pushed out of their homes and forced to live in camps as the wealthy investors built new mansions to live near their gem fields.

A year went by, and then scientists predicted that the largest volcano on the island was going to erupt. The mansion owners laughed off the threat. The leaders of the HIV/AIDS colony, however, chartered two ships to take them off the island. Just one day after the ships set sail, a huge earthquake shook the island and lava heaved out of the volcano, destroying all homes and killing most people on the island.

What shocks you the most about this story? Why?

Was justice served in this story? If not, what would justice look like?

Each of the previous three stories was fictional. Yet they are based on stories found in the Old Testament:

Story one: favor causes jealousy. Joseph dealt with extreme hostility from his brothers and was enslaved in Egypt for unjust reasons (Genesis 37—50).

Story two: let my employees go. Moses led the enslaved Israelites, who were abused by the Pharaoh, out of Egypt toward freedom (Exodus 2—12).

Story three: don't look back. The people in Sodom and Gomorrah were greedy and sexually permissive. God punished them by raining fire down on the towns and destroying all their inhabitants. Only one family—who obeyed God and escaped in time—was spared from punishment (Genesis 14—19).

INTENSE INTERIOR

God Weighs In on Right and Wrong

Divide into four groups. Each group read one set of grievances and discuss the questions listed.

Grievance one: neglect of the poor. He who oppresses the poor shows contempt for their Maker, but whoever is kind to the needy honors God. (Proverbs 14:31)

Now listen, you rich people, weep and wail because of the misery that is coming upon you. . . . Look! The wages you failed to pay the workmen who mowed your fields are crying out against you. The cries of the harvesters have reached the ears of the Lord Almighty.

You have lived on earth in luxury and self-indulgence. You have fattened yourselves in the day of slaughter. You have condemned and murdered innocent men, who were not opposing you. (James 5:1, 4-6)

The LORD enters into judgment against the elders and leaders of his people: "It is you who have ruined my vineyard; the plunder from the poor is in your houses. What do you mean by crushing my people and grinding the faces of the poor?" declares the LORD Almighty. (Isaiah 3:14-15)

"Woe to him who builds his palace by unrighteousness, his upper rooms by injustice, making his countrymen work for nothing, not paying them for their labor. He says, 'I will build myself a great palace with spacious upper rooms.' So he makes large windows in it, panels it with cedar and decorates it in red. Does it make you a king to have more and more cedar? Did not your father have food and drink? He did what was right and just, so all went well with him. He defended the cause of the poor and needy, and so all went well. Is that not what it means to know me?" declares the LORD. (Jeremiah 22:13-16)

What is God teaching about injustice in these passages?

What does this injustice look like today?

Grievance two: exclusivity. They served him by himself, the brothers by themselves, and the Egyptians who are with him by themselves, because Egyptians could not eat with Hebrews, for that is detestable to Egyptians. (Genesis 43:32)

The Pharisees . . . asked Jesus' disciples, "Why does your teacher eat with tax collectors and 'sinners'?" On hearing this, Jesus said, "It is not the healthy who need a doctor, but the sick. But go and learn what this means: 'I desire mercy, not sacrifice.' For I have not come to call the righteous, but sinners." (Matthew 9:11-13)

What is God teaching about injustice in these passages?

What does this injustice look like today?

Grievance three: financial corruption/greed. Hear this, you who trample the needy and do away with the poor of the land, saying, "When will the New Moon be over that we may sell grain, and the Sabbath be ended that we may market wheat?"—skimping the measure, boosting the price and cheating with dishonest scales, buying the poor with silver and the needy for a pair of sandals, selling even the sweepings with the wheat. The LORD has sworn by the Pride of Jacob: "I will never forget anything they have done." Will not the land tremble for this, and all who live in it mourn? The whole land will rise like the Nile; it will be stirred up and then sink like the river of Egypt. In that day," declares the Sovereign LORD, "I will make the sun go down at noon and darken the earth in broad daylight. I will turn your religious feasts into mourning and all your singing into weeping." (Amos 8:4-10)

Look! The wages you failed to pay the workmen who mowed your fields are crying out against you. The cries of the harvesters have reached the ears of the Lord Almighty. (James 5:4)

What is God teaching about injustice in these passages?

What does this injustice look like today?

Grievance four: ongoing, permissive sin. In the following directives I have no praise for you, for your meetings do more harm than good. In the first place, I hear that when you come together as a church, there are divisions among you, and to some extent I believe it. No doubt there have to be differences among you to show which of you have God's approval. When you come together, it is not the Lord's Supper you eat, for as you eat, each of you goes ahead without waiting for anybody else. One remains hungry, another gets drunk. Don't you have homes to eat and drink in? Or do you despise the church of God and humiliate those who have nothing? What shall I say to you? Shall I praise you for this? Certainly not! (1 Corinthians 11:17-22)

With eyes full of adultery, they never stop sinning; they seduce the unstable; they are experts in greed—an accursed brood! They have left the straight way and wandered off to follow the way of Balaam son of Beor, who loved the wages of wickedness. . . . If they have escaped the corruption of the world by knowing our Lord and Savior Jesus Christ and are again entangled in it and overcome, they are worse off at the end than they were at the beginning. It would have been better for them not to have known the way of righteousness, than to have known it and then to turn their backs on the sacred command that was passed on to them. (2 Peter 2:14-15, 20-21)

For a man's ways are in full view of the LORD, and he examines all his paths. The evil deeds of a wicked man ensnare him; the cords of his sin hold him fast. He will die for lack of discipline, led astray by his own great folly. (Proverbs 5:21-23)

What is God teaching about injustice in these passages?

What does this injustice look like today?

Doing Right in God's Eyes

God calls for character that reflects the way to advocate for other people. Review these verses as a large group.

> "Teacher, which is the greatest commandment in the Law?" Jesus replied, "Love the Lord your God with all your heart and with all your soul and with all your mind.' This is the first and greatest commandment. And the second is like it: 'Love your neighbor as yourself.'" (Matthew 22:36-39)

> This is how we know what love is: Jesus Christ laid down his life for us. And we ought to lay down our lives for our brothers. If anyone has material possessions and sees his brother in need but has no pity on him, how can the love of God be in him? Dear children, let us not love with words or tongue but with actions and in truth. (1 John 3:16-18)

> God does not show favoritism but accepts men from every nation who fear him and do what is right. (Acts 10:34-35)

> There is neither Jew nor Greek, slave nor free, male nor female, for you are all one in Christ Jesus. (Galatians 3:28)

> Be imitators of God, therefore, as dearly loved children and live a life of love, just as Christ loved us and gave himself up for us as a fragrant offering and sacrifice to God. (Ephesians 5:1)

What actions in these verses represent the "right thing" to do?

How do these verses call us to advocate for one another?

Vibrant action

One Man's "Wonderful Life"

Read the following story, adapted from the book *Holy Discontent* by Bill Hybels. Then discuss the questions that follow.

In the mid-1980s the rock band U2 played at a day-long concert to raise money for Ethiopian famine victims. Soon after that event, lead singer Bono and his wife, Ali, flew to the Horn of Africa and spent a good portion of that summer working at an Ethiopian feeding camp.

Since then Bono has lobbied powerful world leaders for the cancellation of the debt that plagues two-thirds of the world. He's gathered funding to fight the AIDS pandemic in Africa. He's worked diligently to reform trade policy. After seeing the poor in Ethiopia he decided, "I've got to give myself to something more than making records."

What group of people today might God be asking you to seek justice for?

What can you do about it?

What do you think God expects you to do?

TILL WE MEET AGAIN

As you close your time in prayer, pray that

- God gives you a passion for a specific injustice going on in your community
- God gives you the energy and strength to become an advocate for people facing this injustice

Consider one of the following experiments on your own.

- Between now and the next group meeting, read and discuss the letter "Looking Back—in the Future." Discuss your responses with one or two of your group members.

- Read about Harriett Tubman, an average person who went above and beyond to act against injustice. Reflect and journal about whether or not you could you see yourself doing what she did.
- Watch the movie *Instinct,* starring Cuba Gooding Jr. and Anthony Hopkins, with a friend. Discuss how justice is portrayed in the movie.

One Crazy
Learning Experience

Have you ever seen, with your own eyes, or felt, with your own heart, racial discrimination and injustice? Session ten is a chance to do just that. This learning experience takes you outside of your comfort zone and places you in someone else's shoes.

Avoid selecting a setting or activity out of sheer convenience; rather, where possible, step into multicultural settings to observe and feel the experience firsthand. If your group does not have access to a multicultural setting, alternative learning choices are provided. You'll debrief as a group afterward about your experience.

PRIME IDEAS

- Spend a couple of hours at a driver's license facility or local airport. Watch how people of color are treated compared to the majority.

- Visit a multicultural setting, such as a concert, museum or cultural event, and initiate conversation with at least three people of ethnic backgrounds that are different than yours.

- Dress up in shabby clothes, and go to a nice location, such as a furniture store or a movie theater.

- Give a presentation on "thinking about your future career" or some similar topic to an underresourced middle school.

- Spend a day in a nearby city, restricting yourself to a $10 budget and public transportation.

ALTERNATIVE LEARNING CHOICES

Work in groups to research the following topics:

- Review the book *Divided by Faith* by Michael Emerson. Find three to five compelling facts to share with the group.

- Look up information on the nationwide distribution of wealth. Who are the wealthiest people? What do they do? Who are the poorest people? What do they do?

- Look into the life of William Wilberforce. What makes his story significant?

- Research ten historically significant events of the U. S. Civil Rights movement.

- Review the website <withoutsanctuary.org> (covering lynching in America).

DEBRIEFING YOUR EXPERIENCE

- What was it like for you to step outside your comfort zone?

- What did you observe? How were you treated? How were people around you treated?

- What did you notice about race and justice issues specifically?

One Radical Choice at a Time

CHECKING IN WITH GOD: OPENING PRAYER

As you dive into this learning experience, pray with your small group that as a result of this time together

- God will use one person's story to prompt you to think about the importance of having a role model and being a role model for other people
- God reveals to you how the power of the Holy Spirit can empower you as you seek to stand up for justice and racial reconciliation

OUTRAGEOUS IDEAS

One Radical Choice at a Time: Am I Ready?

Have one group member read the following section aloud. Then answer the questions as a group.

> *Kathy's story.* When I was young, little girls weren't as involved in sports as they are today. You didn't see girls playing softball or soccer. They leapt through dance classes, played with Cabbage Patch dolls and watched *Sesame Street* and *Zoom.* Not me. At five years old, I was regularly outside playing team sports and hanging out with the boys in my neighborhood.
>
> Some parents on our block thought it was strange that I actually had fun hanging out with the boys. One mom in particular thought I was too tomboyish and not feminine enough. Her comments and glances didn't matter to me. The guys in my neighborhood were

surrogate family, especially since my older brother and sister—five and eight years older—were off doing their own thing.

I lived in a relatively quiet and safe suburb of Chicago. My block had its moments though. One high school kid in particular, Danny, often sped down the street in his clunker of a car. He was a known troublemaker; the local cops knew him by name. The kids in the area were all afraid of him—except for Bob.

One day, when Danny was peeling rubber on his car tires, my friend Bob stood right in front of Danny's moving vehicle to make him stop. Danny got out of his car and yelled names at Bob. Inches from Danny's face, Bob, as a young preteen, yelled back. He lectured Danny about speeding down a side street where lots of kids are playing. I remember I never saw Danny speed down our block again.

Bob was like a big brother and role model to me. He inspired me; I wanted to be like him. He taught me the right way to throw a football and wash a car. He celebrated when I did well in softball. More importantly, he challenged my thinking. He'd ask me tough questions about choices related to friendships and other life decisions. Once, I remember him saying, "Just because you're old enough to date, doesn't mean you date everyone that comes your way, does it?"

Another boy on our block, John, wasn't very well coordinated or athletic like the rest of us. He got teased a lot or left out. I took John under my wing and included him in things we did and let him hang out with us. Once, two of my friends started teasing him; I got so mad that I chased them and tried to wrestle them down to the ground. During this physical tumble I yelled, "Don't pick on someone weaker and smaller than you. It makes you bullies. That's mean." They laughed. Later that night, these two guys rang my doorbell and apologized for their behavior. I forgave them, but I wanted them to apologize to John too. From that day on, John was treated with as much respect as his fellow neighbors could muster.

When you were young, who did you want to follow and why?

What is attractive to you about Bob's character?

How did Kathy respond to his character?

Intense Interior

Feeling Others' Pain: God's Gift

Read the following information silently, and then discuss your responses to the following questions in pairs.

Television miniseries captivated me as a child. Not quite reality shows, the dramas brought a shocking slice of truthful history to my young eyes. Two that most intrigued me were *Roots* (about the African American experience) and *The Blue and the Gray* (about the U.S. Civil War).

Seeing people chained, tortured and persecuted because of their skin color shocked me to the core. I wondered, *Where is God in all this?* Although I believed in Jesus and thought of God as compassionate, I limited his compassion toward the sick.

Even though I had a diverse group of friends, I had some fear about minorities. My mind was crowded with stereotypes as I was afraid to drive through lower-income neighborhoods. My parents cautioned me not to drive through certain urban areas. With this warning and no clear rational thinking, I concluded that there was something "bad" about minorities and I could get "hurt."

As I graduated high school and began working, I got my first corporate job at a large, international company located in an upper-class suburb. Many people I worked with had limited or no exposure to people of different races or religions. During one lunch conversation a woman I worked with, with an air of superiority, made random critical comments about "those Jews" and "Blacks." I was so mad—my heart jumped to my lips. "Do you *know* any Jewish or Black people?" I asked. Dumbstruck, she sheepishly answered,

"No," and the conversation ended. From that day on, I was excluded from this woman's clique, and we cordially avoided one another.

Traveling became a consistent part of my job. My first trip was to a small German town. Having dinner with a colleague one night, I was in a position where no one spoke English. I felt high anxiety, knowing I couldn't communicate with people around me. I felt isolated and wanted to be with people "like me." I remember thinking, *This must be what it feels like to be a minority in the United States.*

Another trip was to Puerto Rico. Dining with several women from across Central and South America, I was the only white American present. The conversation turned to race and prejudices. People confided that they had a bad image of white Americans; I asked for details. Alejandra shared how for the longest time her only experience with white Americans was seeing them come to Mexico for spring break. The young visitors often acted liked complete idiots— getting drunk and obnoxious. They'd be disruptively rude, teasing the local people and acting like royalty. It was heartbreaking to hear that, for years, she assumed all white Americans were this way. She didn't want them to come to her country at all.

It was hard to hear that assumptions were made about me because of the pathetic behavior of others in my race. It was healing to share how we transfer our hurt feelings onto people of the same race as those who hurt us. When we ended the conversation, there was genuine appreciation for the opportunity to meet and learn about one another.

Think back to your earliest memories of when you realized people aren't treated the same. How did this make you feel?

VIBRANT ACTION

Kathy's Story: Acting on God's Call

Regather into two groups. Take a few minutes to read the section below; then discuss the questions that follow.

At one point, I was asked to participate in a week-long learning experience called the Justice Journey. A spiritual learning experience through the southern United States, the Justice Journey challenges participants to see the truth about racial prejudice and social injustice, and clearly exposes the devastation that hatred caused during the Civil Rights era. Feeling pressure at work, I was hesitant to commit. Yet I could sense the Holy Spirit nudging me through encouragement from friends and leaders, so I committed anyway. I think this will go down as one of the best decisions of my life.

For four years in a row, I contributed to the Justice Journey as a content developer and small-group facilitator. The first year on the Journey, I took photos. At each historical location or museum, the Caucasian Americans were shocked at the atrocities committed against African Americans. My second year on the Journey, an African American church joined my mostly white church on the learning experience. Some of the most memorable times were when I had chances to talk with African Americans. I clearly remember an African American member saying that he gets glances of mistrust throughout the day because of his color. He described a time when a policeman gave him a hard time for no reason—just because he "looked like" a crime suspect. He expressed the tension of what it feels like just walking out his front door.

This conversation was a marker moment. I thought, *I have no idea what this fear must be like. It is easier for me as a white person. I don't have to worry about being mistreated or mistrusted every day.* This conversation prompted me to consider that, as a white person, I need to go out of my way to build relationships with African Americans. Why would they reach out to me, a Caucasian, if they think we all don't trust them?

Describe a time when God opened your eyes to something he wanted to teach you. How did he invite you to follow him in that teaching?

What is God teaching you now about racial reconciliation and justice?

Following Jesus Radically

Through this serving an extraordinary thing happened—I got to know Jesus better. Jesus had a side to himself that I never knew about. I began to learn how Jesus values women and all people. I've learned at each serving decision point that Jesus doesn't want me on the sidelines living a cushy, "blessed" existence of abundance where I focus on my comfort and ignore the hurting and marginalized people around me. He wants me to surrender to him and follow him *into* ministry. He wants me to live like he did and do what he did.

I've been places in my ministry that I never expected: serving and praying with underresourced people in the city, traveling overseas to build into compassion ministries, educating people on matters of race and justice. I never thought I'd go down the road I have. Whenever I think I don't have energy or time to take the next step, the Holy Spirit gives me the strength to keep going.

As I share my ministry activities with colleagues and friends, they don't always know what to do or say. I think they worry that I am a religious fanatic. As they get to know me, they realize I'm a regular, normal person who has a clear faith. People are drawn to me, as I was drawn to Bob and then Jesus.

My friend Tara feels the same way I do about justice issues. She's an atheist who was exposed to a lot of hypocrisy and judgmental attitudes from Christians in her youth. Tara thinks Christianity is oppressive. She has built trust in me over time and has actually attended church with me more than once to serve at relief efforts or participate in a service about HIV/AIDS. I'm hoping that Tara and other friends like her see my faith in action. When they see I get my conviction and strength from Jesus, my prayer is that they decide to follow him too.

How are your actions appealing to Christians and non-Christians?

Kathy probably never expected her ministry world to grow so large. Yet she took one step at a time. What is the step God is asking you to take today?

What dots can you connect in your life pattern? Where is God calling you?

TILL WE MEET AGAIN

As you close your time together, pray that

- God will give you new insight about how he uses our hunger for justice and racial reconciliation to reveal his presence in our world
- your confidence increases in the role God wants you to play in his plan to increase justice and racial reconciliation in our broken world

At your next and final session, you'll spend time discussing how God is calling you to continue your pursuit of radical Christianity. Between now and then, pray daily about how God is calling you to compassion, justice and racial reconciliation. Ask the Lord, "How can I partner with you to show radical Christianity to a hurting world? How can our group join together to extend our hands of compassion, justice and racial reconciliation outward to others?"

Writing My Story

Am I a Radical Christian?

CHECKING IN WITH GOD: OPENING PRAYER

As you dive into this learning experience, pray with your small group that as a result of this time together

- God increases your awareness of his radical heart for justice, compassion and racial reconciliation
- God moves you to consider ways to live out radical Christianity

OUTRAGEOUS IDEAS

Introductory Remarks for My Autobiography

Many bestselling books have forewords written by influential people. The opening remarks typically affirm the author's character or ideas. When a famous person endorses the author, interest and excitement about the story increase significantly.

Your heavenly Father wants to be a champion for your life story. Break into pairs and restate the Scripture assigned to you in your own words. Limit your paraphrase to one or two sentences.

He has showed you, O man, what is good. And what does the LORD require of you? To act justly and to love mercy and to walk humbly with your God. (Micah 6:8)

Paraphrase:

The Father of compassion and the God of all comfort . . . comforts us in all our troubles, so that we can comfort those in any trouble with the comfort we ourselves have received from God. (2 Corinthians 1:3-4)

Paraphrase:

For you created my inmost being; you knit me together in my mother's womb. I praise you because I am fearfully and wonderfully made. (Psalm 139:13-14)

Paraphrase:

How great is the love the Father has lavished on us, that we should be called children of God. (1 John 3:1)

Paraphrase:

By this all men will know that you are my disciples, if you love one another. (John 13:35)

Paraphrase:

"For I know the plans I have for you," declares the LORD, "plans to prosper you and not to harm you, plans to give you hope and a future." (Jeremiah 29:11)

Paraphrase:

His purpose was to create in himself one new man out of the two, thus making peace, and in this one body to reconcile both of them to God through the cross, by which he put to death their hostility. (Ephesians 2:15-16)

Paraphrase:

Having believed, you were marked in him with a seal, the promised Holy Spirit. (Ephesians 1:13)

Paraphrase:

Speak up for those who cannot speak for themselves, for the rights of all who are destitute. (Proverbs 31:8)

Paraphrase:

That our God may count you worthy of his calling, and that by his power he may fulfill every good purpose of yours and every act prompted by your faith. (2 Thessalonians 1:11)

Paraphrase:

Write down each other's translations in the space below, in the order provided by your facilitator (see p. 147). In place of pronouns such as *you, they* or *us,* insert your own name. A message will form that shows you God's care and plan for you.

Dear Publisher,

_____ (insert your name) is my most
treasured child.

1. _____

2. _____

3. _____

4. _____

5. _____

6. _____

7. _____

8. _____

9. _____

10. _____

Sincerely,
The One who knows _____ the best,
God—on the Eternal Best Selling Author List

What are the key words out of this message that affect you the most?

What do you think about God's purposes for you?

How do you feel knowing that this is how God sees you?

How does knowing that your strength comes from the Holy Spirit motivate you to become an instrument of God's compassion, justice and racial reconciliation?

INTENSE INTERIOR

Stories Live On

God, the perfect communicator, uses story after story in Scripture to illustrate his vision for us. Jesus spent much of his time teaching through telling stories. And over the past twelve sessions you've discussed several real-life stories. Review the summary sentence about each story and discuss the following questions with your group.

A cleansing compassion. Amber's life was painful, self-absorbed and in disarray. God's compassion toward her changed her heart and her actions toward others.

Compassion and frustration: two sides of one coin. Kate was thrown into a family situation where multiple people, including her, needed compassion.

One wave follows another. Alyssa sparked an action-oriented chain of compassion, among children in her school for tsunami victims.

Radical relationships. Nona's compassion for her dying friend Barbara opened the door for other people to extend care to Barbara as they served her prior to her death.

A hidden camera. Sabina, a Muslim woman wearing a jihab, or head scarf, is refused service at a local bakery. Some people defend her, some defend the bakery clerk, but worst of all, most do nothing.

Moments of truth. Sam Chand, John Perkins, Noel Castellanos and Brent Zuercher each share their stories of how personal struggle was overturned by God's power to reconcile through inquiry, awareness and repentance.

When "sorry" isn't enough. Marion Jones cheated and lied, and then paid a high price as a consequence.

One man's wonderful life. Bono has made a significant impact on global poverty and treatment of HIV/AIDS in Africa by leveraging what he has to offer.

Sacrifice one day at a time. Kathy learned that following Jesus means following him into justice and racial reconciliation, which in turn draws people to her.

Which story had the most impact on you? What was it about the story that affected you?

Vibrant Action

Outlining My Crazy-Enough-to-Care Plan

Take a few minutes on your own to write down your responses to these questions. Then rejoin your group, and discuss ways that your group can move forward to creatively seek compassion, justice and racial reconciliation opportunities.

Outrageous Ideas

What topics do you need to understand better or know more about?

How will you increase your knowledge in these areas?

Intense Interior

What attitudes or beliefs do you want to shift?

How will you do this? What support do you need from others?

Vibrant Action

What will you do to live out compassion, justice and racial reconciliation?

Who can you invite to be an accountability partner?

TILL WE MEET AGAIN

As you close this learning experience, pray that

- you become certifiably crazy about caring for other people

- you experience God deeply as you follow Jesus

Complete the prayer request by filling in the blanks below. Tear out the request, and turn it in to your group facilitator.

O Lord, I thank you for what you have taught me through *Crazy Enough to Care!* I am specifically grateful for:

_____

_____

As I look toward the future and listen to your promptings, I ask that:

_____

_____

Most sincerely,

_____(write your name here)

Optional Group Planning

As a group, consider developing a proactive plan for extending hands to others.

- Ask the Holy Spirit to guide your group in a discussion about whether God may be prompting the group to move in a specific direction with your time, talents and resources.

- Brainstorm possibilities for extending compassion, justice and racial reconciliation as a group.

- Create a plan together. Assign roles and tasks throughout the group.

- Organize ways to implement your group's plan. Share duties and responsibilities. Connect regularly and share information.

- Stay committed to your goals and vision. Identify a member who is willing to lead activities for your group.

To get your group started, review these lists of potential areas where you can make a difference. Think about what passion areas and people groups make your heart beat fast. To really delve into your group's next steps, consider scheduling another time to enhance your plan.

PASSION AREAS

Hunger

Poverty

Chronically Ill/Disease

Diversity/Bridge Building

Prison

Widows/Children

Elderly

Homeless/Refugees

Social Justice

PEOPLE GROUPS

International

National

State/Regional

Urban Areas

Church/Small Group

Family/Friends/ Neighborhood

RESOURCES

First Draft of a Plan

1. We will pray about our collective role in reflecting:

_____

_____

2. We feel God is calling us to:

_____

_____

3. Steps toward this calling:

_____

_____

4. Individual team members roles:

_____

_____

5. We will stay connected by:

_____

_____

6. _____ will lead us in keeping this vision alive.

7. Frequency with which we want to serve:

_____

_____

Leader's Guide

INTRODUCTION

The goal of *Crazy Enough to Care* is to increase compassionate acts, acts of justice and racial reconciliation in our churches, communities and world. This learning experience calls us to personally understand and experience God's heart for compassion, justice and racial reconciliation. God invites us to join his work in our world. Upon completion of this learning, the goals are for group members to

- understand the biblical definition of compassion, justice and racial reconciliation

- own the value God places on compassion, justice and racial reconciliation

- experience giving or receiving compassion, calling for justice and extending hands in racial reconciliation

- take a next step to make radical Christianity a lifestyle choice

GAINING PERSPECTIVE

For the purposes of this study, below are three contextualized definitions that lay the foundation for your learning.

Compassion is an active and visible witness of Jesus' followers living out their faith by stepping into and alleviating the pain and suffering of people near them in everyday life and around the world.

Justice is calling out and righting the wrongs that result from the sins of discrimination, exclusivity, oppression, neglect of the poor and economic corruption that leads to poverty.

Racial reconciliation is an authentic and deliberate attempt to bring creation back to its original design by restoring racial harmony and unity among people from different races in a godly fashion.

PROCESS

This learning experience is different from most small-group Bible studies. Each sequential session builds in learning and intensity. Since radical Christianity is all about action, that's what this learning experience encourages. You will find opportunities throughout this course for hands-on learning.

Real time learning. The sessions are to be completed in the group setting. Members are not asked to do work before coming to the small-group meeting, although they're given follow-up opportunities at the end of each session. Writing space is limited in favor of encouraging spontaneous group discussion. Therefore time and space are important elements to consider with this curriculum. Consider what meeting time, duration and setting are best to encourage fruitful discussion.

Action-based serving experience. Learning professionals agree that people grow the most when they "learn by doing." Imitating Jesus' behavior is a strong catalyst for personal growth and change. Each session has activities to keep small-group members engaged in the learning process and includes true, real-life stories of compassion, justice and racial reconciliation.

"Getting out of the house" is an important component to radical Christianity. To challenge your group, we have two external activities woven into this learning experience. Session four directs your members to leave the safe and predictable small-group environment and move toward areas of compassionate service. A few weeks prior to the actual serving experience begin thinking about where your group may serve. Planning a few weeks ahead gives you the necessary time to make the appropriate contacts and arrangements for an effective serving experience.

Session ten offers another "getting out of the house" learning experience. This session gives your group an opportunity to experience racial discrimination and justice issues firsthand.

Learning format. This learning experience seeks to invite God's transformation of our minds, hearts and actions. In the participant guide, the concepts *outrageous ideas, intense interior* and *vibrant action* are referenced. Group members are asked, in the introduction, to consider these questions:

The OUTRAGEOUS IDEAS of Jesus. How can Jesus transform my mind? How do I see things the way Jesus does? How can Scripture be my guide? What are my blind spots when it comes to God's fullest plan for my life?

An INTENSE look at my own INTERIOR. How can Jesus transform my emotions? How could the things that break God's heart break my heart?

The VIBRANT ACTION God is calling me to take. How can Jesus transform my actions? If Jesus were in my shoes, how would he respond to people near me?

The prayers and activities provided in "Till We Meet Again" will help you build on what you learned as a group in between sessions. In addition, sessions four and ten are opportunities to experience what you've learned in a real-world environment.

SESSION PLANNING

Since this learning experience includes activities and stories, it is extremely important for you to review your Leader's Guide a couple of days before your small-group meeting. At times, you need to prepare materials or topics prior to the meeting.

This Leader's Guide provides coaching on

- session time and length
- objectives
- materials needed
- process flow
- alternate group discussion questions

The participant guide includes key verses, stories, questions and activities. In the following session-objective chart, the learning objectives are presented as questions.

SESSION TITLES AND LEARNING OBJECTIVES SUMMARY

Session 1: God's Radical Heart-Change Plan	Learning Objective
Outrageous Idea	How is God compassionate? Do I see God as compassionate?
Intense Interior	Do I realize God wants me personally to experience his compassion?
Vibrant Action	Am I open to seeing myself the way God sees me?
Session 2: Neighbors Close to Me	Learning Objective
Outrageous Idea	How does God define neighbor?
Intense Interior	Do I recognize that people near me are in pain? How do I want to react? Am I willing to engage in another person's painful experience?
Vibrant Action	How do I see others? How does God call me to show compassion to my neighbors?
Session 3: The People Jesus is Especially Crazy About	Learning Objective
Outrageous Ideas	Do I know that God has a compassionate heart toward specific people? Who are they? What does he tell us about serving them?
Intense Interior	How am I willing to obey God and move toward the people he is especially crazy about?
Vibrant Action	How does God call me to extend myself to care for and serve the neglected and oppressed people in society?
Session 4: Extending My Hands	Learning Objective
	To provide a hands-on experience where members encounter God by serving other people as he calls us to in Matthew 25.
Session 5: Relationships That Reflect God's Compassion	Learning Objective
Outrageous Ideas	What is God challenging me to learn about compassion through this story?
Intense Interior	How do I feel about the sacrifice needed to reflect compassion in this circumstance?

Vibrant Action	What impact does this story have on my actions? How can I expect God to replicate my actions? Will my trust in God's replication power impact my actions?
Session 6: God's Love for Variety	**Learning Objective**
Outrageous Ideas	Do I see the prevalence of prejudice and exclusivity in our world? Have I grasped that exclusive behavior is unbiblical?
Intense Interior	How am I personally exclusive or inclusive? Do I recognize when I am inclusive or not?
Vibrant Acton	Am I ready to own and confess the ways that I have excluded, judged or minimized the value of other races?
Session 7: God's Call to Cross the Divide	**Learning Objective**
Outrageous Idea	What is God's plan for reconciliation? What does he expect of us?
Intense Interior	Am I wiling to cross racial divides?
Vibrant Action	Am I humble enough to apologize or forgive?
Session 8: Exploring Justice for All	**Learning Objective**
Outrageous Idea	What is justice and injustice in God's eyes?
Intense Interior	What is my experience with injustice?
Vibrant Action	Have I accepted Jesus' death on the cross as God's act of justice?
Session 9: A Radical Righter of Wrongs	**Learning Objective**
Outrageous Ideas	What is justice and injustice in God's eyes?
Intense Interior	Do I recognize when people near me are treated unjustly? What do I do when I see injustice happen to others?
Vibrant Action	How does God call me to be an advocate for justice?
Session 10: One Crazy Learning Experience	**Learning Objective**
	To provide an opportunity to experience racial discrimination and/or justice issues firsthand.
Session 11: One Radical Choice at a Time	**Learning Objective**
Outrageous Ideas	When Jesus says, "Come, follow me," what do I think he wants me to follow him into?

Intense Interior	How willing am I to obey Jesus' lead?
Vibrant Action	How do my actions draw people to Jesus?
Session 12: Writing My Story	**Learning Objective**
Outrageous Ideas	How does God invite me to follow him?
Intense Interior	What learning have I absorbed into my heart through this study?
Vibrant Acton	Who is God calling me to be? What is God calling me to do as result of this study?

YOUR ROLE AS LEADER

Your group's desire to embark on a compassion, justice and racial reconciliation journey speaks volumes about your group. This experience proves to be challenging and very rewarding at the same time. As a leader in your group, think of yourself:

As a follower. Lean on the Holy Spirit to guide you. It will be important for you to pray and plan before leading each session. You can be a conduit to assist people in seeing the truth of God's great plan:

It is important for the Holy Spirit to do the convicting during this study. No member should feel shame about his or her past action or inaction regarding compassion, justice and racial reconciliation. In positioning yourself as a co-learner, you have the opportunity to model a healthy sense of obedience, vulnerability and dependency on God.

Show and share what you are learning. As you model authentic sharing, you will give others permission to learn (to be wrong, to discover, to risk) and create a lasting bond for the group as a whole.

As a facilitator. Your role is to keep discussion flowing and keep things on target. There are times when you need to be bold and confront your group. There are times when you need to be patient and sensitive. It is important to help instill a healthy sense of vulnerability during discussion.

Trust the Holy Spirit. You know your group members. There may be moments, after you read a story or Scripture, when a time of silence is best. Be open to what God is doing in the moment. This study provides discussion questions as tools for you; the Leader's Guide further offers questions for "Going Deeper." They have a bit more zing and challenge to them. Feel free to adapt your questions to fit the needs of your group.

As a friend. One of your roles in this experience is as a friend to your members. You are experiencing this journey along with them. You have an opportunity to grow as a leader on this journey.

Sometimes needs arise that go beyond your area of expertise. At this time, your most appropriate response is to assist a member in connecting with someone who is formally trained such as a counselor, elder or care minister.

EXTENDING HOPE

God has a deep love for all his children. Jesus wants us to be his eyes, heart and feet to this hurting world. Living a radical Christian lifestyle moves all of us one step closer to the fully surrendered life to which God calls us.

Session One: God's Radical Heart-Change Plan

Outrageous Ideas. How is God compassionate? Do I see God as compassionate?

Intense Interior. Do I realize God wants me to personally experience his compassion?

Vibrant Action. Am I open to seeing myself the way God sees me and accepting his compassion?

Material preparation required: none.

SECTION & TIME	OBJECTIVE & MATERIALS	PROCESS & CONTENT
Open 5 minutes	Welcome the group and create a friendly, safe environment to begin sharing.	*Prayer:* Check in with God through an opening prayer. Direct group to pray in the direction of the noted bullet points.
Outrageous Ideas 15-20 minutes	*Objective* To set context and get in the right frame of mind prior to diving into session one.	***An Exercise in Compassion:*** Compassion is . . . The goal of this activity is to build a baseline understanding of how the group defines *compassion*. **Note:** At the end of the learning experience, you'll revisit the compassion definition, so make sure you keep a copy of your final definition from this session.

103

SECTION & TIME	OBJECTIVE & MATERIALS	PROCESS & CONTENT
Outrageous Ideas (continued) 15-20 minutes	*Materials Needed* • Large paper the size of a flip chart • Markers or colored pencils, one for each session *Objective* To understand the integral nature of compassion in God's character.	Follow instructions in participant guide to create definition. Give group members positive feedback on their compassion definitions. Highlight how each of us may define *compassion* a little differently. Raise awareness and expectation about how the group will learn and grow in the definition of compassion during this experience. If it would help your group visually, draw the graphic below on your flip chart, and fill in the "spokes" with the words people use to describe compassion. **God's Autobiography** Have each group member take a turn to read aloud one of the verses about God, and facilitate discussion of the questions in the large group setting. ***Jesus—Living, Breathing Proof of God's Compassion*** Either read this content to the group or assign someone in the group to read it out loud *Going Deeper* • How does receiving compassion from God make you feel? • What are the positive feelings? • What are the confusing or negative feelings that come with being on the receiving end of compassion?

Section & Time	Objective & Materials	Process & Content
Intense Interior 30 minutes	*Objective* To personally understand whether or not I am open, like Ms. Amber, to receiving God's compassion.	***A Cleansing Compassion*** Have members read this story silently or out loud in groups of two or three, and answer the questions in the participant guide. *Going Deeper* • What is your reaction to Amber's story? • What affects you most about her story?
Vibrant Action 30 minutes	*Objective* To learn whether or not I am open to seeing the need for compassion all around me. *Materials Needed* • Scissors • Pens	***Receiving God's Compassion*** Either read this content to the group or assign someone to read it out loud ***Keeping a Close Watch*** Ask group members to fill out the bookmark in their participant guide. This brief exercise assists them in connecting with the assignment before leaving the meeting. Have them • jot down moments when they have experienced God's compassion • cut the bookmark from the page • keep the bookmark with them in their wallets, calendar, back packs or briefcases between now and the next session • bring the bookmark to the next meeting, even if it is tattered and worn
Till We Meet Again 10 minutes		There is a lot of value to reinforcing the main points of this session in a closing prayer. Encourage group members to go deeper by considering these activities. The news exercise in particular will help people to prepare for the next session on neighbors. • Memorize one of the verses in the section "God's Autobiography." • Watch a newscast or read a newspaper. Is compassion a character trait that is valued in society? Why or why not?

Session Two: Neighbors Close to Me

Outrageous Ideas. How does God define neighbor, and what is my responsibility to my neighbor?

Intense Interior. Do I recognize when people near me are in pain? How do I want to react? Am I willing to engage in another person's painful experience?

Vibrant Action. How do I see others? How do I show compassion to other people? How does God call me to show compassion to my neighbors?

Notes. This session opens up some excellent opportunities for you as a leader:

- Since session two is all about people close to us, this is a great time to talk about giving compassion within the context of your small group. You have an opportunity to model healthy vulnerability, as well as invite it from others.

- Compassion is a response to people who are in all types of pain or need—emotional, physical or spiritual. You can discuss addressing physical versus emotional and spiritual needs throughout the learning.

- Consider which activities work best in your group. Were there any distractions last session? How can you try to eliminate or minimize these?

- If there are topics especially interesting or urgent for your group right now, think of ways to bring them into the discussion. You may have compassion needs in your group right now. Or, there may be situations in your church body or neighborhood that can be highlighted in this session.

Material preparation required: none.

SECTION & TIME	OBJECTIVE & MATERIALS	PROCESS & CONTENT
Open 10 minutes	*Objective* To set context and get in the right frame of mind prior to diving into session two content.	*Summarize* key points from session one. *Discuss:* How did the bookmark exercise impact you? How did your awareness of compassion increase? By summarizing the key ideas from session one and reviewing the bookmark activity, your group members build a base of understanding that they can use in session two. Use this time to address questions or misconceptions. *Pray* together as a group before you delve into the activity. Use the prayer prompts in "Checking In with God."
Outrageous Ideas 30 minutes	*Objective* To consider each person's ability to notice compassion opportunities, views about giving compassion and the assumptions/biases about what kindness people deserve.	**Someone's Dialing 911—Do You Pick Up?** Here, group members stretch their awareness of compassion needs and call out the various ways people respond to them. Break people into three groups so that they can discuss one scenario per group. Answer the questions in the smaller group setting. *Going Deeper* • What do you do if you are not sure if someone is sincere about his or her needs (you suspect dishonesty or manipulation)? • What do you do when you believe someone's poor choices are the cause of his or her current difficulties?

SECTION & TIME	OBJECTIVE & MATERIALS	PROCESS & CONTENT
Intense Interior 30 minutes	*Objective* To translate a popular biblical story into modern-day language as a way to increase the impact of the compassion story. *Materials Needed* • Paper and pencil	***Walking by a 911 Emergency*** *Read:* Bring your members together; read them the parable of the Good Samaritan while they listen silently with their eyes closed. Ask the group to imagine the story as if it happened today. Encourage silence so members have a few minutes to let their imaginations kick in. After inviting them to open their eyes, invite them to share who they pictured as characters in the story. What character did each group member become? Why? Discuss the impact of this reflection exercise on members. What did they learn about themselves? ***Compassion and Frustration—Two Sides of One Coin*** Read this story out loud together and answer the discussion questions as a large group. *Going Deeper* • What person in this story would you have the most trouble showing compassion to? Why? • How do you react when you are asked for advice and the person doesn't take it?
Vibrant Action 15 minutes	*Objective* To increase personal sensitivity and awareness of people near you in need.	***My Compassion Challenge*** Pair group members up to share their current challenges that are stretching them beyond their compassion capacity—a compassion challenge. If individuals do not have current challenges, they can use past situations as items to discuss. *Going Deeper* This activity can be done in place of the compassion challenge exercise. Consider this exercise if • your group knows one another fairly well or has been together for a long time • you sense members are open and vulnerable

SECTION & TIME	OBJECTIVE & MATERIALS	PROCESS & CONTENT
Vibrant Action (continued) 15 minutes		• you know they will act beyond the group meeting Lead a discussion regarding how people feel about • their own abilities to give compassion • how the group responds to one another's needs • how they respond to needs outside of the group *Probing Questions* • On a scale of 1-5, with 1 as poor and 5 as excellent, how effectively do you identify and respond to others' needs for compassion? How do you know this about yourself? • On a scale of 1-5, how well do we show compassion within our group? • Discuss examples of compassionate serving within the group (celebrate it). • Discuss examples of times when a compassionate serving opportunity within the group was missed. Why was it missed? • What compassion needs to exist within this very group now?
Till We Meet Again 5 minutes	*Objective* To continue a personal process of discovery and learning.	In this session, you'll see the increase in intensity of "Till We Meet Again" from session one. Adapt the prayer points as necessary. What does your group need the most from God right now? Pray that. *Remind group members* of the suggestions for personal reflection in the guide, along with additional learning resources if they want to do more on their own. Encourage your members to choose one of these activities on their own time. You can gently yet boldly stress that members get out of the learning what they invest in it.

Session Three: The People Jesus Is Especially Crazy About

Outrageous Ideas. Do I know that God has a compassionate heart toward specific people? Who are they? What does he tell me about serving them?

Intense Interior. How am I willing to obey God and move toward the people he is especially crazy about?

- Do I care about people most oppressed in our society?
- Do I trust God and believe that I can make a difference in their lives?
- What heart issues do I have that get in the way of my reaching out to the oppressed, marginalized and underresourced?

Vibrant Action. How does God call me to extend myself to care for and serve the neglected and oppressed people in my society?

Notes. This section doesn't have "Going Deeper" questions because the "Roads to Compassion" activity encourages deep reflection. The whole discussion is an exercise in going deeper.

Material preparation required:

- Remove the "Society's Opressed ad Marginalized Worksheet" from the participant guide (p. 32) to use as a master for recording group responses.
- Remove the "Exploration Card Worksheet" from the Leader's Guide (p. 116), and cut along the lines so that you have one question on each card.
- Session four is an experiential serving activity. Read session four participant and Leader's Guide instructions. Consider serving experiences that will work for your group. Discuss possibilities with the group at the end of this session to get input. Be sure to let the group know how and when you will finalize plans with them.

SECTION & TIME	OBJECTIVE & MATERIALS	PROCESS & CONTENT
Open 5 minutes	*Objective* To set context and get in the right frame of mind prior to diving into session processing and planning.	*Summarize* key points you would like to highlight from session two. *Discuss* people's experience with the "Till We Meet Again" activity. How would the group gauge its compassion? High or low? Why? *Pray* together as a group before you delve into the session. Use the prayer prompts in "Checking In with God."
Outrageous Ideas 30 minutes	*Objective* To understand that God has a special love for the oppressed in our society and wants others to love and care for them as he does. *Materials Needed* • Flip Chart	***Just a Train Ride*** The purpose of the icebreaker is to explore our assumptions and feelings about people who are different, especially those less fortunate than ourselves in one way or another. Read the short scenario about an imaginary train ride together. Either have individuals read the situation on their own or you can read it to the group. Discuss the questions posed after the scenario. ***Stops Along the Way*** The purpose of this Scripture is to get a glimpse of Jesus' behavior toward the oppressed and marginalized. Through the questions provided, the group will explore Jesus' interactions with the oppressed and discuss how he models an active faith to his followers. Ask people to gather in pairs or groups of three to read the Scripture passages. You may want to assign the verses so that each of them is read and referenced. Ask the pairs to discuss the questions. *Notes on Scripture* Encounter 1: Zacchaeus was a tax collector. Tax collectors were despised at the time. They were often unethical—imposing more taxes than required so they could get rich. They had few friends and were considered traitors in their day.

111

SECTION & TIME	OBJECTIVE & MATERIALS	PROCESS & CONTENT
Outrageous Ideas (continued) 30 minutes		Encounter 2: There was a major political and religious rift between Jews and Samaritans. Samaritans had a Jewish background but mixed with another religion and practiced in pagan and unorthodox ways. In some cases, Samaritans were killed as a way of racial cleansing. In addition to being a Samaritan, the woman at the well was married five times and was currently with a man who was not her husband. This behavior from a woman was clearly a social disgrace. Encounter 3: Women in Jesus' day were highly oppressed. They had no control over their lives or decisions—men were responsible for them (e.g., husbands, fathers, uncles). There were many practices in place that prohibited Jewish men from interacting or communicating with women. In addition, the women who followed Jesus were especially unique: some were diseased, some were possessed and some were wealthy (it was uncommon for women to have money, let alone the freedom to spend it as they pleased).
Intense Interior 30 minutes	*Objective* To explore our personal experiences, beliefs and actions as they relate to the most oppressed and marginalized in our society today.	***Roads to Compassion (Part 1)*** After the pairs have had enough time to discuss the questions from "Stops Along the Way," discuss their responses to the final question as a large group. List the answers in the squares on the "Society's Oppressed and Marginalized" worksheet (p. 32). Place only one answer per box. Each box should have a person/group of people who are oppressed or marginalized in today's society. Fill in all the squares, even if you have to repeat a response in more than one square. Provide additional insight as needed. You will use this filled-out sheet for the second part of the "Roads to Compassion" activity.

SECTION & TIME	OBJECTIVE & MATERIALS	PROCESS & CONTENT
Intense Interior (continued) 30 minutes	*Materials Needed* • Question Card Worksheet • Scissors *Prep Before Session* Cut question card deck so you have twenty-five questions, one per card.	***Roads to Compassion (Part 2)*** The goal of this exercise is to explore personal experiences and beliefs in a safe setting and then to apply your understanding of how God calls us to act today. The following statement is in the participant guide; be sure you read it to the group. We all have different levels of experience, interest and beliefs about the people who are marginalized and oppressed in our society. Our experiences may range from "I am unfamiliar with life situations different than mine" to "I am overwhelmed by the issues certain people face" to "I seek out opportunities to support people who are marginalized." Pull out the "Exploration Cards." There should be twenty-five total cards with one question on each. *Instructions for Exercise* • Each participant is to draw a card from the deck and answer the question as openly as possible. • Participants may "pass" once, if they so choose, no one should be forced to answer. • Each person may have a maximum of one minute to read, think about and answer the question. Use an egg timer or watch to time the responses. • Allow each person at least one turn. Exercise should not exceed 30 minutes.

SECTION & TIME	OBJECTIVE & MATERIALS	PROCESS & CONTENT
Intense Interior (continued) 30 minutes		The purpose of this discussion is to acknowledge the barriers we face personally and socially when it comes to intentionally caring for the most oppressed and hurting people in our world today. After the "Exploration Cards" activity, ask people to turn to the "Roadblocks to Compassion" chart in the participant guide (p. 32). Ask the group to describe, in three words or less, what stops them from compassionately reaching out to the most hurting and oppressed. Ask everyone to fill in the chart with the group's responses. Everyone may not want to actually write the words in their participant guide; that is OK. You want to ensure that you capture the roadblocks on the flip chart. You may want to reference this information later in this session or in future sessions.
Vibrant Action 30 minutes	*Objective* To understand God's expectations of us regarding the most oppressed and marginalized in today's society. *Materials Needed* • Flip chart	***Delete Fear—Insert Faith*** Consider asking the group to take turns reading portions of the information out loud. When complete, consider summarizing the importance of every action offered to God by serving the oppressed and marginalized. Emphasize that one small act of faith can be multiplied and used by God to show his glory. Many people are reached in the process. If time permits, provide a real example from your own life where you have experienced this power of "miraculous multiplication." Acknowledge that others may have similar experiences. Encourage group members to overcome their roadblocks—even when they feel their action won't make much of a difference. God is all powerful and sees what we don't. He will use everything we offer in big and small ways. ***One Wave Follows Another*** Read the real life story "One Wave Follows Another" to the group. Discuss questions.

Section & Time	Objective & Materials	Process & Content
Till We Meet Again 5 minutes		The next session in this adventure is a group serving opportunity. As you close your time together, pray that • you grasp God's vast love toward people in serious need and his replication power made available to us as we step up to serve • you prepare your mind, heart and hands for your upcoming serving opportunity Affirm the work your group has done to this point in *Crazy Enough to Care*. Prepare your group for the learning experience: 1. Share with the group a compelling vision for the serving experience. The vision may come from either your personal experience or through a story. 2. Provide a few options for where the serving experience could happen. Provide all necessary details and clarify how any follow-up details will be communicated. 3. Talk about the connection between your church and the sites being considered for the serving experience. This helps build confidence in the hearts of the volunteers. 4. Ease group members' minds regarding safety issues and other barriers that could hinder the serving experience. 5. If there are financial costs involved in the serving experience, state them up front; don't catch your group members off guard. Encourage people to try the exercises in the "Till We Meet Again" section of the guide.

Roads to Compassion Activity, Part 2
Exploration Cards Worksheet

Photocopy this page and cut out the cards in advance of the session.

Explore How would you motivate the people in box R4?	**Explore** Do you believe it is possible to rid society of the cause of the misfortune for the people in box S3?	**Explore** When was the last time you interacted with someone represented in box O2?	**Explore** What is God saying to you now, in this moment about the group of people represented in box A1?	**Explore** What perceptions do you have about the group of people in box O5?
Explore Tell about a time you reached out to the people in box R1?	**Explore** How hard would it be for you to reach out and serve the people represented in box D4?	**Explore** What tangible wish do you have for the people represented in box H3?	**Explore** What stops you from reaching out to the people in box A3?	**Explore** What difference do you believe you can make by reaching out to the people in box S1?
Probe Deeper What would you do if you were suddenly in need and someone in box H1 offered to assist you? What would you think/feel?	**Probe Deeper** How would you react if someone in box R3 invited you over for dinner?	**Probe Deeper** Tell what happened when you last interacted with people represented in box A4?	**Probe Deeper** Tell which group of people on the grid your heart "beats fast for" and why.	**Probe Deeper** Tell which of the groups on the grid would be most difficult for you to reach out to and why.
Probe Deeper If you could rewind time and replay your last interaction with a person in box H5, what would you change?	**Probe Deeper** What act of compassion could you show to the group in box O1?	**Probe Deeper** What would you have to sacrifice to show compassion to the people in box S2?	**Probe Deeper** How do you believe the people in box O3 would respond to your assistance?	**Probe Deeper** Explain how you have been blind to the struggles of the group in box D2?
Discover What is a stumbling block that prevents you from reaching out to the people in box D5?	**Discover** Describe a time when you felt God used your heart to reach out to one of the groups in this chart?	**Discover** If you were forced into one of these circumstances yourself, which would you dread the most and why?	**Discover** What is one thing Jesus would do for the people in box S4?	**Discover** What would you like to learn about the people in box S3?

Session Four: Extending My Hands

Notes. A group serving experience gives your members an opportunity to experience compassion first hand. There are mutual benefits in serving. By proactively assisting people in need, your members become the hands and feet of Jesus to the people they serve. It is important to know that through a serving experience your group may receive much more than they give. They experience God as they serve.

You may schedule your serving experience to happen in place of a typical meeting, or you may schedule your experience during your fourth session. Connect with your church leaders for ideas on how to best serve in your particular community or region, but be sure to choose what is best for your group. You can also consider the suggestions below.

You may decide to send your group out in teams of two. Or you may choose to experience one event together. Use your discernment on what will challenge but not intimidate your group.

Material preparation required: none.

SERVING DAY	CONTACT PERSON/ LOCATION	ACTIVITY OPTIONS
	Objective To experience the power of a compassionate serving experience as a group activity.	**Observing Team Readiness** Make a mental assessment of where your team is at on the topic of serving. • How did the team react to the idea of serving? • If the reaction was positive and eager, why are they eager? • What types of serving opportunities is the group considering? • Which members seemed a bit apprehensive about serving? Why? If your group seems apprehensive about serving, you may have trouble gaining momentum and energy in the group. So you may want to consider selecting the serving opportunity yourself. If the group is open, however, you can work together to creatively brainstorm serving opportunities.

SERVING DAY	CONTACT PERSON/ LOCATION	ACTIVITY OPTIONS
		You may run in to resistance as you prepare to serve. There are times people are skeptical of serving because they feel assisting others in a bad situation hinders the person or keeps them "stuck." How do you handle this hesitancy? There really is no right or wrong answer. Boundaries in serving are a topic people need to wrestle through. You may chose to • pray with the group or person struggling • go back to the roadblocks in section three to discuss why he or she is struggling • encourage members to push through their doubts and see what the actual serving experience is like and if their thoughts or feelings change as a result Success factors in a good serving experience include • team prayer before the serving experience • clarity on the goal of serving experience • preparation for the new environment and experience as the team serves diverse and underresourced people • a connection to the group you are serving • clear communication on the time, day, location you are serving • awareness of and preparation for any safety issues • transportation to the event for all team members • appropriate tools or supplies • sharing of responsibility • debriefing and prayer to process the serving experience

Serving Day	Contact Person/ Location	Activity Options
		Processing Questions A key success factor is debriefing as a group as soon as possible. Once you complete your serving time, allocate at least thirty minutes to process the experience with your members. Ask them the following questions: • What were your first impressions during your serving interactions? • What was it like to interact with people who are in a different situation than you? • Did your impressions/feelings change over the serving time? How? • What took you out of your comfort zone? • What did you learn the most? • How did you experience Jesus in the moment? • What is Jesus telling you through this experience? • What defining moment did you experience while serving? The next session will explore how friendships across boundaries can be made deeper.

Session Five: Relationships That Reflect God's Compassion

Outrageous Ideas.	What is God challenging me to learn about compassion through this story?	
Intense Interior.	How do I feel about the sacrifice needed to reflect compassion in this circumstance?	
Vibrant Action.	What impact does the Barbara and Nona story have on my actions? As I commit to serving others with compassion, how can I expect God to replicate my actions?	
Notes.	• This session focuses on a real-life story of two women, each in need of compassion, and a small group that showed up to serve them.	
	• God's replication power is highlighted in the ripple effects of this story of friendship, love, compassion, bold acts of service and evangelism.	
	• The story is separated into four sections with featured discussion questions.	

Material preparation required: none.

Section & Time	Objective & Materials	Process & Content
Open 10-20 minutes	*Objectives* To set context and get in the right frame of mind prior to diving into session six processing and planning.	*Summarize* key points from the serving experience. If you haven't had a chance yet to debrief from your experience, allocate at least twenty minutes to discuss the debrief questions noted in the leader's notes for session four. *Pray* together as a group before you delve into the session. Use the prayer prompts in "Checking In with God."
Outrageous Ideas 30 Minutes	*Objective* To be challenged, through this story, to see the results of deep compassionate sacrifices and the spiritual and relational results of these compassionate actions.	***A Friendship in Need*** State the following introduction to the group: • The call to radical compassion includes the call to radical relationships. When we seek to live like Jesus, we connect with all kinds of people with a variety of needs. Sometimes we can directly assist them. Or our role may be to introduce them to Jesus, the God of compassion who wants to meet their needs.

SECTION & TIME	OBJECTIVE & MATERIALS	PROCESS & CONTENT
Outrageous Ideas (continued) 30 Minutes		• The following is a true story of how an everyday small group began to make an eternal impact for God with their neighbors. It all begins with a woman named Barbara. Read section one to the group yourself, or pick someone in the group who you know is comfortable reading aloud. *Going Deeper* • What level of sacrifice could you make for a friend? • What might stop you from serving? Lack of time, energy, finances, emotional connection?
Intense Interior 20 Minutes		***A Neighbor—Becoming a New Friend*** Split your group into pairs to read section two silently and then discuss the questions. *Going Deeper* • What do you fear most about approaching someone you don't know well? • Why do you have that fear? ***A Friendship Circle Grows*** Form two groups. Read the section below out loud, and then have each group discuss the questions that follow. Ask someone from each group to facilitate the discussion. *Going Deeper* • What do you truly believe about God's faithfulness to you as you step out and serve others in his name? • How do you expect that he will be there for you?

SECTION & TIME	OBJECTIVE & MATERIALS	PROCESS & CONTENT
Vibrant Action 10 minutes		***Contagious Compassion Impacts Long-Term Serving*** Reconvene as one group. Ask someone from the group to read the last section. Discuss the questions. *Going Deeper* • Whose job is it to reach out to lonely, hurting people? • Do hurting people have a responsibility to reach out for help?
Till We Meet Again 5 Minutes		Close your time in prayer using the prompts in the participant guide. Evangelism is difficult for some people. During the first group serving experience, members may not have been comfortable sharing their faith as they served. With another serving experience coming up, encourage team members to begin seeing how they can use their actions to share their faith as the small group did with Nona. Reference items in the "Till We Meet Again" section for growing in evangelism. The sessions now shift to delicate issues such as discrimination and prejudice. Spend some time before your next session praying for you and your group about the tough discussions to come about divides among ethnic groups and classes in our society.

Session Six: God's Love for Variety

Outrageous Ideas. Do I see the prevalence of prejudice and exclusivity in our world? Have I grasped that exclusive behavior is unbiblical?

Intense Interior. How am I personally exclusive or inclusive? Do I recognize when I am inclusive or not?

Vibrant Action. Am I ready to own and confess the ways that I have excluded, judged or minimized the value of other races?

Material preparation required: none.

SECTION & TIME	OBJECTIVE & MATERIALS	PROCESS & CONTENT
Open 10 minutes		*Summarize* key points you would like to highlight from session five. Focus on content that was particularly influential for the group. Ask if anyone created an "elevator" speech for sharing their faith. Have one or two group members share their one-minute version. *Pray* with your small group using the prompts in the participant guide. *Discussion* This discussion reveals what people think about race in our society. Does race matter or not? Ask the question below, and give enough time for members to respond. If you encounter silence, don't rush in with additional questions. Use probing questions as needed. Acknowledge and summarize some of the points you hear people make. Limit the discussion to ten minutes, explaining that your discussion is a social experiment. This is meant to warm people up to the topic of the session and needs to go quickly. • Does race matter in our society? If so, to what degree? *Going Deeper* • Describe a time when you have seen discriminatory treatment? Where were you? What happened?

SECTION & TIME	OBJECTIVE & MATERIALS	PROCESS & CONTENT
Outrageous Ideas 50 minutes	*Objective* To understand that race matters in society and it doesn't matter to God.	***A Hidden Camera*** This activity works through a potential situation, and members are to honestly discuss how they may react. After the group discussion, summarize what actually happened in the social experiment done by *ABC Primetime News.*
		Assign three group members to read the dialogue. Instruct them not to read one another's lines ahead of time. Have them play out their lines in the moment— impromptu.
		Ask the rest of the group members to imagine they are customers in their favorite bakery. They are observing the encounter but do not speak up at all. After the reading, allow fifteen minutes for discussion, and then summarize what happened in the real social experiment. After discussion, read the following.
		The real Muslim woman watching in the van was interviewed about her reactions to the patrons' responses. She was *surprised* that anyone actually defended the Muslim woman/actress. She thanked them and shared tears with them. She was *not surprised,* however, by the other responses. She shared that it's those responses that scare her the most. It's why she never goes anywhere alone, no matter what the time of day.
		Going Deeper • Which of these three responses would you have most likely had? • How do you feel about that?
		Transition to a discussion of what God thinks of all this by asking the now common question, "What would Jesus do?" The purpose of this discussion is to understand what Scripture says about exclusion and inclusion of races.
		You have fifteen minutes for this discussion. Ask people to break into pairs and read through the biblical messages in the guide and answer the questions noted.

SECTION & TIME	OBJECTIVE & MATERIALS	PROCESS & CONTENT
Intense Interior 20 minutes	*Objective* To explore how race matters to each person individually.	***Rewinding the Tape*** This activity assists members in reflecting on their own attitudes, beliefs and actions related to race. Encourage authentic exploration and honest acknowledgment. Explain that the activity is an individual exercise with a few general questions for group discussion. People are not expected to share detailed results of their reflection time unless they want to. Direct members to identify where they are at on the racial awareness continuum—deny, know, challenge or participate. If space allows, encourage people to disperse in the space available so they can be alone and have some privacy. Say a short prayer to get the group in the right frame of mind. *Prayer Points* Ask God to open the group's hearts to see what he sees. Ask for honest reflection about personal attitudes about race. Ask for willingness to change so that we consistently respond as Jesus would. After twenty minutes, gather the group back together and lead them through the confession exercise in the next section.

SECTION & TIME	OBJECTIVE & MATERIALS	PROCESS & CONTENT
Vibrant Action 10 minutes	*Objective* To confess personal sin related to racial discrimination.	***Dialing God's Number—Steps Toward Oneness*** This prayer/confession exercise acknowledges that race matters in ways that do not honor God and his plan for the body of Christ. Transition into the exercise by explaining that members have a time of confession. Explain that no matter where members are individually on the continuum of racial reconciliation, each person needs to collectively confess to God that race matters in the church and society as a whole. Race does matter and it shouldn't. Repentance is a very important step toward real racial reconciliation. We cannot reconnect and make things right if we don't acknowledge the wrong. Acknowledge that some group members may have asked for forgiveness in this area in the past, while others may still be struggling with the idea that race matters. Suggest that these members participate in the prayer by listening or praying silently. Ask the members to respond silently as you lead them through the prayer prompts. Feel free to customize these prompts to meet the needs of your members. *Suggested starter statements:* • Acknowledge: God, I have been exclusive toward other races by . . . • Repent: Father, my thoughts and behavior toward other races do not line up with your behavior for me as a Christian. I show this by . . . • Seek forgiveness: Father, please forgive me for . . . I want to be more like you by doing . . .

Section & Time	Objective & Materials	Process & Content
Vibrant Action (continued) 10 minutes		*Suggested closing prayer points:* • We acknowledge that race matters more than it should in our world and in our lives personally. • We may not always see things the way you do, nor do we always respond the way you do when it comes to race. • We repent; We are part of a broken world and are affected by it one way or another. • We ask your forgiveness, and we thank you for the grace and mercy that you offer. • We ask you to help us see things the way you do and give us courage to respond the way you do when it comes to race. *Going Deeper* If your group is comfortable being vulnerable, ask them to pray out loud as they respond to your prayer prompts.
Till We Meet Again 5 Minutes		Close the session in prayer. Reference the activities listed in "Till We Meet Again" to encourage people to go deeper on this topic. Remind people that the topic of racial reconciliation will be continued in the next session. Recommend that group members watch *In My Country* with a friend or family member before the next session in order to better understand the racial divide.

Session Seven: God's Call to Cross the Divide

Outrageous Ideas. What is God's plan for reconciliation? What does he expect of us?

Intense Interior Am I willing to cross racial divides?

Vibrant Action. Am I humble enough to apologize or forgive?

Material preparation required: none.

Section & Time	Objective & Materials	Process & Content
Open 5 minutes		*Summarize* the key points from the previous session. Ask group members to discuss ways they observed that race matters since the last session. Be careful not to let the discussion detour. *Pray* as a group, using the prompts in the participant guide.
Outrageous Ideas 60 minutes	*Objective* To understand God's view of reconciliation.	**Gracious Moments of Truth** The stories in this section are powerful, real-life examples of people who went through a process of racial reconciliation. The following discussions draw out biblical principles about the process of reconciliation. The group splits into four subgroups. Each group reads a story about racial reconciliation and discusses it. The four groups will have twenty minutes for this activity. After twenty minutes, gather the large group together to summarize key learnings from the stories. Ask each group to • summarize the story in a nutshell • discuss one or two takeaways about the reconciliation process (what attitude, behaviors or process elements were required) Allow approximately five minutes per group (twenty minutes total).

SECTION & TIME	OBJECTIVE & MATERIALS	PROCESS & CONTENT
Outrageous Ideas (continued) 60 minutes		*One Minute Away from Expulsion—Samuel Chand* *Wounds That Go Deep—John Perkins* *A Long Walk—Noel Castellanos* *Unexpected Learning—Brent Zuercher* Summarize key elements of the reconciliation process by reading through "What Makes Reconciliation Work?" (inquiry, awareness and repentance). Discuss the questions noted with the group (twenty minutes). *Going Deeper* • Which of these key elements of reconciliation is easiest for you? Why? • Which is hardest? Why?
Intense Interior 15 minutes	*Objective* To explore how I feel about racial reconciliation.	***Crossing the Divide Called Fear and Distrust*** This personal reflection exercise assists members in processing how they can apply the learnings from the stories and discussion to their own hearts. Each person does his or her own letter to God privately. Ask the group to individually write their own "letter across the divide" using the sentence starters provided in the guide.
Vibrant Action 15 minutes	*Objective* To pray for reconciliation between races and for personal growth in the area of racial reconciliation.	***One Prayer Closer to Unity*** The purpose of this activity is to close the time in prayer, while also providing a visual representation of the issues around racial reconciliation. Ask everyone to stand together in a close circle. Challenge them to get close, while respecting the personal space of others. Have some fun with it. Once everyone is together, make positive remarks about the group as you transition into prayer. For example, "We are so blessed to be in this group learning together. God smiles as we learn and are challenged together. Aren't we an awesome group?"

SECTION & TIME	OBJECTIVE & MATERIALS	PROCESS & CONTENT
Vibrant Action (continued) 15 minutes		Share the following, or similar, prayer points and instructions: • God, we thank you for bringing us together to learn about your Word and your expectations about racial reconciliation. We have joy in community although we are wrestling with challenging material. God, we acknowledge once again that race matters more than it should in our world and in our lives. • (Ask the group to turn their backs toward one another and step away from one another so they are no longer touching and then direct them to close their eyes.) The way we are standing now represents the brokenness, shame and distance that we experience when we are exclusive. God, we ask you to help us see things the way you do. • (Ask the group to come back to their starting position, huddled close together.) God, this is what we hope you see when you look at us—one family, your family in community, regardless of race. Amen.
Till We Meet Again 5 Minutes		Reference the activities listed in "Till We Meet Again" for the group members who want to go deeper on this topic. Because the topic may be new to people and the content is intensifying, the activities are particularly helpful preparation for the next session.

Session Eight: Exploring Justice for All

Outrageous Ideas.		What is justice and what is injustice in God's eyes?
Intense Interior.		What is my experience with injustice?
Vibrant Action.		Have I accepted Jesus' death on the cross as an act of God's justice?
Notes.		Justice is a complex biblical concept. The design of the sessions about justice is kept at an introductory level. The general flow of the two sessions on justice is as follows:

> What do I think about justice?
> How do I feel about justice?
> What does God think about justice?
> How does God feel about justice?
> What does God do about justice?
> What do I do about justice?

Material preparation required:

- Tear out the page in the Leader's Guide (p. 137) for the activity: "Justice or Not."

- Cut the word table along the lines to have a set of cards for the activity.

- Session ten is an experiential learning activity. Read session ten participant and Leader's Guide instructions. Consider learning experiences that will work for your group. Get input from the group at the end of this session. Be sure to let the group know how and when you will finalize plans with them.

SECTION & TIME	OBJECTIVE & MATERIALS	PROCESS & CONTENT
Open 5 minutes		*Summarize* key points from the previous session.
		Pray together as a group before you delve into the session. Use the prayer prompts in "Checking In with God."
Outrageous Ideas 30 minutes	*Objective* To understand the group's views related to justice.	***At the Tip of My Tongue*** Take ten minutes for this activity, the purpose of which is to discuss what justice currently means to the group. This activity is meant to go fairly quickly to start the process; it is not meant to lead to a definition that everyone agrees with.

131

SECTION & TIME	OBJECTIVE & MATERIALS	PROCESS & CONTENT
Outrageous Ideas (continued) 30 minutes		Reference the word-association worksheet (p. 61). Ask people to check off the words that they associate with *justice.* Provide a few minutes for them to do this individually.
		After people are finished, ask for a volunteer to share the words he or she chose and why. Ask another person to share who chose different words. Ask a third person to share who chose yet different words.
		Summarize what you heard. Transition to the next activity by explaining that the group is going to review their personal experience with justice.
		Jesus—the Ultimate Advocate Take ten minutes for this discussion. The purpose of this discussion is to reflect on biblical principles related to justice so that the group can gain a closer understanding of God's heart on the matter. Read the introduction and Scripture referenced in the participant guide. Discuss the questions with the group.
		When Saying "I'm Sorry" Isn't Enough Take ten minutes for this activity. The purpose of this story is to share a public example of someone who made mistakes in life, causing others pain.
		Read and discuss the Marion Jones story with the group. If you prefer, ask for a volunteer to read the story.
		Going Deeper Think of a time you made a big mistake. How did you feel? Was an apology enough? Did the consequence match the action?
		Summarize Transition by acknowledging that justice is complex. There are two strong perspectives when a wrong is committed.

Section & Time	Objective & Materials	Process & Content
Outrageous Ideas (continued) 30 minutes		• When we are victims of injustice, we are angry and expect justice. The person wronged wants consequences for bad choices. Often the person wronged doesn't feel justice is fully served. • When we are the ones who make a bad choice and inflict injustice on others, we are ashamed and want mercy. We want to be forgiven. We don't want to suffer consequences. • Our human nature is not sufficient to be objective—therefore, we need an intermediary to protect both sides.
Intense Interior 30 minutes	*Objective* To understand the group's personal experience and emotions related to injustice.	***Justice or Not*** The purpose of this activity is to reflect on the group's personal experience related to justice. You'll want to draw out people's emotional responses to experiencing personal injustice (anger, frustration) and the injustice they've inflicted on others (shame, embarrassment, disappointment). Remove the activity page (p. 137) and cut the squares into individual cards. Each card should have a sentence starter on it. • Place the cards in the middle of the group. • Ask one person to pick a card. Have this person read the card and complete the sentence. • If he or she can't complete the sentence, have the card passed to the person on the left. Keep this pattern going until someone can answer the question. If no one can answer the question, place the card to the side. Start again with another card. • When someone completes a question, ask the probing questions from the participant guide. • After the question is answered, have the next person pick a card. Repeat instructions above. • Continue picking cards until time runs out for the exercise. Depending on the length of people's responses, there may not be time for everyone to respond.

SECTION & TIME	OBJECTIVE & MATERIALS	PROCESS & CONTENT
Intense Interior (continued) 30 minutes		• If the group is vulnerable, consider adding a twist to the exercise. Ask people to share when they've committed a wrong against someone verses sharing when they were wronged. Summarize what people feel when they are victims of injustice. Point out that not only are we victims, we are victimizers. There are times we cheat, lie and hurt others. Share an example from your own experience. *Example:* I really let my son down recently. I told him if he mowed the lawn each week over the summer, I would go on a week-long camping trip with him. For a variety of reasons I wasn't able to hold up my end of the deal. I felt very bad about this. He was upset for a long time; I can tell he lost some trust in me. We want things to be set right when we are victims. We want mercy when we are victimizers. When we are forgiven, we experience a tremendous sense of relief and gratitude because we know we messed up.
Vibrant Action 30 minutes	*Objective* To understand and reflect on Jesus' crucifixion as an act of ultimate justice by God.	**Shocking Penalty** The purpose of this reading and discussion is to understand the impact of Jesus' crucifixion as God's sacrifice to bring reconciliation and justice to the human race. God sent Jesus to earth to pay the ultimate price of our sins, a moment of justice for God. Through the Holy Spirit's presence, he also commands us to bring justice to the world—the main focus of the next session. Read the poem by Marie Guthrie. Speak slowly and pause after each period. Read the poem a second time to allow people to process. Transition by reading John 3:16-18 to the group. Summarize the gospel of Jesus Christ:

SECTION & TIME	OBJECTIVE & MATERIALS	PROCESS & CONTENT
Vibrant Action (continued) 30 minutes		• As a God of justice, from the beginning he had consequences and judgments for the sins of humans. • For years, humans tried to reconcile their sins through their own efforts, through sacrifices and rituals to please God. • Because of his love for us, God did not want us to suffer these harsh judgments. • He sent his one and only Son, Jesus Christ, to be with us, teach us and ultimately sacrifice himself for us. • When we accept and believe in him, his sacrifice pays the price for our sins and gives us a new life for here and eternity. You may have people in the group that have not understood this truth before. They may commit or recommit themselves to Christ as a result of understanding this fact. Many times people make a faith decision silently or only reveal the action to another person privately. To lead someone in a prayer to accept Christ, cover a couple of simple prayer points: • The person should acknowledge sin in his or her life and that Christ is needed as his or her savior. • The person should acknowledge that Christ died and rose again to cover his or her sin. • The person should ask Jesus to lead his or her life. • The person should thank God for his gift of grace and forgiveness. You may have followers who have not understood the concept of Jesus' death as a moment of justice for God, and this fact may raise deep questions for them. Answer the questions as best you can. If necessary, suggest that you engage in deeper conversation offline. If you get questions you can't answer, be up front and say you need to do a little homework. Seek information and counsel from trusted members of your church.

SECTION & TIME	OBJECTIVE & MATERIALS	PROCESS & CONTENT
Till We Meet Again 5 minutes		Close the session using the prayer points noted. Encourage group members to go deeper by considering further how Jesus' death was a payment for your wrongdoings and mistakes. In what sense might Jesus' death be all about justice from God's perspective? Session nine is intentionally heavy on Scripture. Be sure to review the definition of justice and the Scripture readings in advance of the next meeting. Alert the group to the serving experience slated for session ten. As a leader, you will need to decide whether you will select the group activity or if you want group consensus.

Activity: Justice or Not Starter Cards

Photocopy this page, then cut along the gridlines to make a deck of sentence starter cards.

I was cheated...	I was really hurt when ...	I was lied to ...	I can't stand it when people are treated like ...
I was robbed ...	I was wronged when ...	My workplace treats people inconsistently when ...	The worst time I was teased ...
I got angry at the customer service I received when ...	The contractor for my house project didn't deserve payment ...	My close friend disappointed me when ...	I should have gotten ...
I was discriminated against ...	I was threatened when ...	Someone close to me got exposed to drugs ...	I was owed money but was not repaid ...
The car accident was not my fault ...	My parents were taken advantage by ...	My child did not fulfill a commitment ...	My child was hurt by ...
The drunk driver hit me ...	My neighbor ruined our relationship by ...	I could not believe it when the cop ...	My church was not honest when ...
The school should not have ...	I was physically wounded ...	The gang in my neighborhood ...	My government took advantage of me ...
Can you believe ...	Can you believe ...	Can you believe ...	Can you believe ...

Session Nine: A Radical Righter of Wrongs

Outrageous Idea.   What is justice and injustice in God's eyes?

Intense Interior.   Do I recognize when people near me are treated unjustly? What do I do when I see injustice happen to others?

Vibrant Action.   How does God call me to be an activist for justice?

Notes.   The content in this session is the most challenging in the study to date. Keep your group focused on the topic of justice. Stay patient if you find that people have trouble grasping justice in today's scenarios. Do not feel rushed to move along for the sake of time.

Material preparation required:

- Read the participant and Leader's guide instructions for session ten. Finalize plans for your group experience at the end of this session.

SECTION & TIME	OBJECTIVE & MATERIALS	PROCESS & CONTENT
Open 5 minutes	*Objective* To open the session and focus the group on the topic at hand.	*Summarize* key points you would like to highlight from session eight. Focus on content that was particularly influential for the group. Ask about group members' insights and reactions to the concept that the cross is symbolic of God's justice. *Pray* together as a group before you delve into the session. Use the prayer prompts in the participant guide.
Outrageous Ideas 30 minutes (10 minutes per story)	*Objective* To understand God's view of justice.	***Happily Ever After—NOT*** The purpose of this activity is to understand what justice is in God's eyes. Ask for volunteers to read each of the three stories to the rest of the group. After each story is read, discuss the questions below fairly quickly—only one or two responses per story. After discussing the last story, summarize the biblical stories for the group.

SECTION & TIME	OBJECTIVE & MATERIALS	PROCESS & CONTENT
Intense Interior 35 minutes	*Objective:* To explore God's direction to each of us personally regarding how we should respond to injustice.	***God Weighs In on Right and Wrong*** The purpose of this activity is to understand Scripture as it relates to very common injustices to which we can all relate. Also, the questions open up the opportunity for the group to discuss what God is asking us to do about these injustices. Divide people into four groups and assign each group to one of the sets of Bible passages in the four grievances. Ask each group to read the passages and answer the questions noted in the participant guide. The groups have fifteen minutes to read the passages and discuss the questions. *Going Deeper* • Which of the grievances we covered is a sin you struggle with or are tempted by? • How do you overcome it? After fifteen minutes, ask the groups to come back together. Now discuss the verses that God shares about character that is right in his eyes. Take twenty minutes for this discussion. See also the following: Micah 6:8 Proverbs 31:8-9 Proverbs 22:22-23 Proverbs 11:25 Amos 5:24
Vibrant Action 20 minutes	*Objective* To discuss how God may be calling you to be an activist.	***One Man's "Wonderful Life"*** Read the story about Bono to the group. Discuss the questions that follow.
Till We Meet Again 5 minutes		Ask God to open the group's eyes to injustice and to give the group courage and willingness to step out in faith against injustice in the world. Communicate details of the upcoming learning experience/activity and clarify how any follow-up details will be communicated.

Section & Time	Objective & Materials	Process & Content
Till We Meet Again (continued) 5 minutes		1. Share with the group a compelling vision for the serving experience. The vision may come from either your personal experience or through a story. 2. Provide a few options for where the serving experience could happen. Provide all necessary details and clarify how any follow-up details will be communicated. 3. Talk about the connection between your church and the sites being considered for the serving experience. This helps to build confidence in the hearts of the volunteers. 4. Ease group members' minds regarding safety issues and other barriers that could hinder the serving experience. 5. If there are financial costs involved in the serving experience, state them up front; don't catch your group members off guard. Encourage group members to try the activities listed in "Till We Meet Again."

Session Ten: One Crazy Learning Experience

This session gives your group an opportunity to experience racial discrimination or justice issues first-hand. This learning experience takes group members outside of their comfort zones by giving them opportunities to step into someone else's shoes. As much as possible, your group is encouraged to encounter multicultural settings so that they can observe and feel the experience firsthand. If you do not have access to a multicultural setting, you have alternative learning choices.

Schedule your learning experience to occur during a typical meeting, or use your meeting time to choose a time for the experience.

You may find it productive to pair people up and send members on different learning experiences. Or you may desire to have one experience for your entire group for team-building purposes. Your goal is to challenge, not intimidate your group; use your discernment on the best option for your members.

Material preparation required: none.

SERVING DAY	CONTACT PERSON/ LOCATION	ACTIVITY OPTIONS
	Objective To experience racial discrimination and injustice issues first hand.	**Observing Group Readiness** Assess how well your group responds to stepping outside their comfort zone. Ask yourself: • How does the team react to the learning experience idea? • If the reaction is positive and eager, why are they eager? • What type of learning experience is the group considering? • Which members seem a bit apprehensive about the experience? Why? If your group is apprehensive about stepping outside their comfort zone, you may want to consider selecting the learning experience for the group. A hesitant group may have trouble gaining momentum. If the group is open, however, work together to select one of the learning experiences or create your own customized experience. Ensure that you are not forcing an experience on team members who are uncomfortable, and keep the experience to the time for only one team meeting.

Section & Time	Objective & Materials	Process & Content
		Focus on • placing yourself in a multicultural setting • moving outside your comfort zone (avoid selecting a setting out of sheer convenience) There are several options for the learning experience listed in the participant guide. Success factors for having a good learning experience include • team prayer prior to activity • clear goals and well-thought-out objectives • preparation and coaching regarding a new environment • clear communication on the time, day and location • awareness and preparation regarding any safety issues • transportation to event for all team members • debriefing and prayer after the learning experience ***Processing Questions*** Once you complete your learning experience, debrief with your group by discussing the following: • What took you out of your comfort zone? • What did you learn the most? • What is Jesus telling you through this experience? Have people prepare for the next session by thinking about times they've had to make difficult decisions. • What made the decision difficult? What would be the consequences of a bad decision? How did you feel God leading you in the decision?

Session Eleven: One Radical Choice at a Time

Outrageous Ideas. When Jesus says, "Come, follow me," what do I think he wants me to follow him into?

Intense Interior. How willing am I to obey Jesus' lead?

Vibrant Action. How do my actions draw people to Jesus?

Notes. This session focuses on one woman's story of spiritual growth and obedience in the areas of justice and racial reconciliation. When a Christian is obedient and lives out the values of justice and racial reconciliation, non-Christians are drawn to us. The story is separated into four sections with featured discussion questions.

Material preparation required: none.

SECTION & TIME	OBJECTIVE & MATERIALS	PROCESS & CONTENT
Open 10-20 minutes	*Objective* To set context and get in the right frame of mind prior to diving into session eleven processing and planning.	*Pray* together as a group before you delve into the session. Use the prayer prompts in "Checking In with God."
Outrageous Ideas 30 Minutes	*Objective* To be challenged, through this story, to see the importance of role models, noticing injustice around you, responding to Jesus and drawing others to him through your actions.	***One Radical Choice at a Time: Am I Ready?*** State the following introduction to the group: • The call to radical Christian living calls us to reflect on our life priorities and how God places people in our lives as role models. The following is a true story of how one woman's desire to follow Jesus took her down a serving road she didn't expect. Read section one to the group yourself or pick someone in the group who you know is comfortable reading aloud. *Going Deeper* • Were you drawn to more positive or negative role models in your youth? Why is that?

143

SECTION & TIME	OBJECTIVE & MATERIALS	PROCESS & CONTENT
		• What's wrong with this picture? A young girl accepted by young guys? What do you think was the secret to her success?
Intense Interior 20 Minutes		***Feeling Others' Pain—God's Gift*** Split your group into pairs to read section two silently, and then discuss the questions. *Going Deeper* • How did your family or work experience shape your views of different ethnicities or races? • How important is it for Christians to avoid stereotypical images or misinformation pertaining to people of color? • Have you ever used derogatory language or had derogatory thoughts regarding another race? Why do you think it surfaced?
Vibrant Action 15 Minutes		***Kathy's Story: Acting on God's Call*** Have members gather into two groups. Read the section out loud to the group, and then have each group discuss the questions that follow. Ask someone from each group to facilitate the discussion. *Going Deeper* • What barriers do you face hearing or responding to God's promptings? • Do you currently have any friends of color? If so, how deep do your conversations take you on the subjects of racial discrimination and prejudice? ***Radically Following Jesus*** Ask someone from the group to read the last section to the entire group. Discuss the questions. *Going Deeper* • In what ways do you draw people to God? • In what ways do you push people away from God? • Currently in your walk with Christ, are you a spectator or an advocate for social causes such as compassion, justice and racial reconciliation?

Section & Time	Objective & Materials	Process & Content
		• What does this look like in your daily life? • Are you inviting seekers within your circle to experience underresourced environments along with you? • How are you paying attention to the Holy Spirit as he prompts you to start spiritual conversations with seekers who serve alongside you? Share an example. • To lead people to Jesus is an awesome responsibility. Have you experienced this? What was it like?
Till We Meet Again 5 Minutes	*Objective* To prepare for the final session.	As preparation for the final session ask your group to pray about what God is calling you to do individually, and as a group, to reflect his compassion, justice and heart for racial reconciliation. Ask the Lord • How can I partner with you to live like a radical Christian? • How can my small group join together to extend radical Christianity outward to others? Ask your members to reflect on what extreme sacrifices they would be willing to make moving forward and to jot down any specific thoughts or promptings that they may have in this area. You will work on a plan during your final session together.

Session Twelve: Writing My Story

Outrageous Ideas.	How does God invite me to follow him?
Intense Interior.	What learning have I absorbed into my heart through this study?
Vibrant Action.	What is God calling me or my group to do as result of this study? How can my group and I move into the future crazy enough to care

- in our everyday interactions?
- in a significant serving experience?
- in advocating for societal changes?
- in personal crosscultural relationships?
- in modeling a more inclusive spirit and presence?

Notes.	This session focuses on processing the entire study. Group members take time to form an action plan based on their learnings and God's call for us to follow Jesus' lead individually and collectively.

Material preparation required:

- Have a few pages of flip-chart paper and some bold color markers ready to use.

SECTION & TIME	OBJECTIVE & MATERIALS	PROCESS & CONTENT
Open 5 minutes	*Objective* To set context and get in the right frame of mind prior to diving into session twelve to process and plan.	*Pray* together as a group before you delve into the session. Use the prayer prompts in "Checking In with God."
Outrageous Ideas 25 minutes	*Objective* To remember God is crazy enough to care; he wants us to follow Jesus so that we can be connected with God, join him in ministry and draw others to him.	***Introductory Remarks for My Autobiography*** The goal of this exercise is to summarize the learning in this study. The group takes key Scriptures and turns them into an endorsement letter from God using modern-day language. Reference the Scripture list in the participant guide. Assign Scripture references to individuals or pairs, assigning multiple Scriptures as needed. Order of verses is listed below. The participant guide intentionally references the verses in a different order.

SECTION & TIME	OBJECTIVE & MATERIALS	PROCESS & CONTENT
Outrageous Ideas (continued) 25 minutes		1. "For you created my inmost being; you knit me together in my mother's womb. I praise you because I am fearfully and wonderfully made" (Psalm 139:13). 2. "How great is the love the Father has lavished on us, that we should be called children of God" (1 John 3:1). 3. " 'For I know the plans I have for you,' declares the LORD, 'plans to prosper you and not to harm you, pans to give you hope and a future'" (Jeremiah 29:11). 4. "The Father of compassion and the God of all comfort, who comforts us in all our troubles, so that we can comfort those in any trouble with the comfort we ourselves have received from God" (2 Corinthians 1:3-4). 5. "His purpose was to create in himself one new man out of the two, thus making peace, and in this one body to reconcile both of them to God through the cross, by which he put to death their hostility" (Ephesians 2:15-16). 6. "Speak up for those who cannot speak for themselves, for the rights of all who are destitute" (Proverbs 31:8). 7. "Having believed, you were marked in him with a seal, the promised Holy Spirit" (Ephesians 1:13). 8. "He has showed you, O man, what is good. And what does the Lord require of you? To act justly and to love mercy and to walk humbly with your God" (Micah 6:8). 9. "By this all men will know you that are my disciples, if you love one another" (John 13:35). 10. "That our God may count you worthy of his calling, and that by his power he may fulfill every good purpose of yours and every act prompted by your faith" (2 Thessalonians 1:11). Ask the group to review the Scripture and take a few minutes to summarize, in just one-two sentences, in their own words. When everyone is done, ask the group to share their summaries one at a time. Use the number key to have the summaries read in order. (This is important to ensure the message makes sense.)

SECTION & TIME	OBJECTIVE & MATERIALS	PROCESS & CONTENT
		As people share their summaries, write them on a large piece of flip-chart paper. Don't write too big because you want the whole thing to fit on one page. Before writing the first summary, write "Dear Publisher" at the top. After the last summary, write "Sincerely, the one who knows _____ the best."
		After you have gone through the summaries initially, read the statement in one full swoop to the group.
		Summarize the experience by acknowledging the truth of the words on the page. Let people know that God's words are alive and meaningful, we can count on them and God counts on us to make them real for ourselves.
		Discuss the extreme questions.
Intense Interior 20 minutes	*Objectives* To reflect on the learnings we've had individually and collectively throughout the study.	***Stories Live On*** The purpose of this discussion is to give people a chance to look back over the learning experience and reflect on what had the most impact on them.
		Use the questions in the participant guide. Consider adding some of the following questions that will take you deeper. However, this discussion is meant to only last twenty minutes.
		Going Deeper • What story had the most impact on you? • What story made you uncomfortable? • What story completely took you by surprise? • Describe a key takeaway from one story. • Have you had a similar experience that made you connect personally with one of these stories? • How did God speak to you through one of these stories? How did you experience this? • What did you disagree with or struggle with as we discussed these stories? • In what ways have these stories made you aware of other stories in your family, neighborhood, workplace, etc.?

SECTION & TIME	OBJECTIVE & MATERIALS	PROCESS & CONTENT
		• How has your radar gone up as we've discussed people's personal journeys as radical followers of Jesus?
Vibrant Action 30 minutes	*Objective* To action plan at an individual level based on learnings from the study.	***Outlining My Crazy-Enough-to-Care Plan*** The action planning time outlined here is for individual level reflection and planning. Some groups may have the desire and energy to continue learning or taking action on issues related to compassion, justice and racial reconciliation. If that's the case with your group, you may want to consider using the group planning process provided as a "Going Deeper" option. *Going Deeper: Individual Planning* • Begin with a few minutes of private prayer. Suggest the group ask God to give each individual direction on how he or she may move forward individually. • Give members fifteen minutes to privately think through the list of questions on the "Outlining My Plan" page. • Spend about fifteen minutes having members share highlights of their action plans with the group. • Ask members to take a few minutes to fill out the prayer request card. When they are finished, ask them to tear the card out and hand it to you. These will be used in the closing prayer activity. *Going Deeper: Group Planning* If you choose to do group planning, you will most likely need to set up a separate time with your group. There is not enough time built into this session to cover both individual planning and group planning. Discuss specific ways God is prompting your group to act together in community. Ask members about their desire to collectively extend compassion, justice and racial reconciliation to others. Ask the question: "How could we use our spiritual gifts collectively?" Use the brainstorming lists to prompt ideas. Narrow the list to one-two areas of focus.

SESSION TWELVE

Section & Time	Objective & Materials	Process & Content
		Create a vision/goal statement for your crazy-enough-to-care plan. State a few reasons why this plan is important to the group. Work through a plan on how group members will implement the goal. (Identify to-dos, assign owners and project timing.) Discuss how the group will connect and communicate with one another as the plan is implemented. Keep in mind that someone in your group may have the desire or interest in playing a leadership or administrative role in these activities. Most success occurs when the group owns the next step. Establish other ground rules as needed for group communication, such as providing feedback to one another, supporting one another, reaching out for help, agreeing upon meeting commitments, etc. Discuss the importance of future debriefing sessions.
Till We Meet Again 15 minutes		*Prayer Activity* • Place all prayer cards you received in a pile, or put them in a hat. • Stand in a circle. • Ask each group member to pick one of the cards. If they pick their own, they need to place it back in the pile. • One at a time, ask each person to read the name on the card. This person needs to step into the middle of the circle. • Ask the person who picked the card to move into the middle of the circle as well and become an intercessor for the person by placing a hand on the card owner and praying for his or her needs. • Continue the process until each group member has received prayer. • Close with a commissioning blessing on the group.

6084